Praise for
He Blew Her a Kiss

"Compelling...A source of healing comfort...A great way to strengthen your inner life. *He Blew Her a Kiss, Vol. 2* is hope from start to finish. It will expand your awareness of the mystery of life."

~ Louis E. LaGrand, Ph.D., Author of *Healing Grief, Finding Peace: 101 Ways to Cope with the Death of Your Loved One*

"As the chapter leader of a parental bereavement support group, I find the messages of the *He Blew Her a Kiss* books to be a tremendous source of hope and comfort for parents searching for peace and purpose in their new lives without their beloved children."

~ Betsy Friedl, The Compassionate Friends Memphis Chapter

"HEARTWARMING AND BRILLIANT...Angie and Kelley take us on a compelling journey that no other book on afterlife communication can match. This book is truly helpful to all who read it...that death is not the end!"

~ Glenda Pearson, Certified Grief Recovery Specialist, Author of *But Should the Angels Call for Him: A Mother's Journey through Grief and Discovery*

"This book is a treasure, one that leaves the reader filled with wonder and a warm heart."

~ Chassie West, Author of *No Reasons for Goodbyes: Messages from Beyond Life*

"An amazing, heartfelt collection of experiences that will provide you with a new perspective on life after death, and fill you with the peace, comfort, and hope you are longing for from your loss."

~ Deborah Heneghan, Author of *Closer Than You Think: The Easy Guide to Connecting with Loved Ones on the Other Side*

"Very inspiring book filled with stories of the many ways our loved ones who have crossed over can and absolutely do connect with us."

~ Guy Dusseault,
www.facebook.com/groups/SignsFromOurLovedOnes
www.oursonbilly.com

He Blew Her a Kiss
Vol. 2

TRUE STORIES OF AFTER-DEATH COMMUNICATION, AFFIRMING LOVE SHARED IS ETERNAL

Angie Pechak Printup & Kelley Stewart Dollar

outskirtspress
DENVER, COLORADO

The opinions expressed in this manuscript are solely the opinions of the author and do not represent the opinions or thoughts of the publisher. The author has represented and warranted full ownership and/or legal right to publish all the materials in this book.

He Blew Her a Kiss
Volume 2, True Stories of After-Death Communication, Affirming Love Shared Is Eternal
All Rights Reserved.
Copyright © 2013 Angie Pechak Printup and Kelley Stewart Dollar
v3.0

Cover Image by Angie Pechak Printup & Kelley Stewart Dollar. All rights reserved - used with permission.

This book may not be reproduced, transmitted, or stored in whole or in part by any means, including graphic, electronic, or mechanical without the express written consent of the publisher except in the case of brief quotations embodied in critical articles and reviews.

Outskirts Press, Inc.
http://www.outskirtspress.com

ISBN: 978-1-4327-9106-3

Outskirts Press and the "OP" logo are trademarks belonging to Outskirts Press, Inc.

PRINTED IN THE UNITED STATES OF AMERICA

Acknowledgements

It is important that we express our sincere gratitude to the many people who shared their personal experiences with us. We admire the courage it took for them to open up and allow readers to delve into what was, for many, very private and intimate moments. Only through their willingness to share can others find hope and reassurance regarding the loss of a loved one.

We owe a debt of gratitude to the pioneering work and research about after-death communication conducted by Bill and Judy Guggenheim. We honor and appreciate the time and effort they devoted then and the continued work they do today.

We also thank the growing number of readers who have made the conscious effort to open their hearts and minds to new perceptions of life after death. Through love, compassion, and a willingness to share with others, we can all minister to those suffering from the loss of a loved one.

Finally, special heartfelt thanks to our family and friends. None of this would have been possible without their love and support. They have lifted us up and encouraged us every step of the way, always having believed in what we intended to accomplish. Our love and gratitude extends beyond words.

Dedication

In memory of Tom and Judy McKelroy, whose love for one another reached beyond physical boundaries and touched the hearts of so many. To their son, Jay, whose recent and tragic loss leaves a void in the lives of his family and friends, we know you are safe and happy with your parents again.

In recognition of the pain and loss both have experienced, we also dedicate this book to Jay's sister, Emily, and his wife, Jennifer. Your strength is a true inspiration.

Contents

Foreword i
Introduction v
He Blew Her a Kiss 1
Inspirational Stories 7
    A Nugget of Reassurance 9
    Remembering Ma 15
    In the Line of Duty 23
    Morning Glory! Rise and Shine 29
    A Name Says It All 33
    A Saint's Farewell 39
    The Blessing of a Child 45
    A Promise Kept 49
    Love Shines Bright 55
    Butterfly Kisses 61

A Christmas Spirit of Love 65
A Song of Love 69
The Irises Are Blooming 73
A Father's Love Is Forever 79
The Healing House 87
The Journey Begins 93
Hello, I'm Still Here 101
Fairy-Tale Love 109

Inspirational Stories – Multiple Submissions 113
A Pink Balloon, Please 115
My Hero Forever 119
Love Reflected in a Poem 127
I Can Always Count on Mom 135
Wings of Love 143
Believe in Yourself 149
Never Far Away 153
The Beauty of a Butterfly 163
The Right Choice 171
The Letter 177
A Gift for Grandpa 185
A Ride to Remember 189
New Beginning 195
A Morning Surprise 201

Resources 207
Index 211
About the Authors 213

Foreword

Mention ADC, or after-death communication, to someone and you get any number of different reactions. Some give a snort and dismiss the subject out of hand. Some sidle away quickly, wanting no part of being around a person who is patently insane. Or, they listen politely, nod, and then take a hike with long, hurried strides. Some listen, clearly fascinated and willing to give it some thought. Some truly do embrace the subject and have even experienced their own ADC. And some freeze, mouth hanging open. A sure sign they've experienced something they've never been able to explain and decided to forget it, because doing anything else was too uncomfortable. Ten years ago I admit I would probably have been among the snorters, with absolutely no frame of reference to attach to the phenomenon.

We are raised to believe that death is the end of a life, the big fat period at the end of a sentence. Depending on our religious background, we may rest easy with the concept of a loved one in Heaven, blissfully enjoying its streets of gold, or conversely, ending up well south of the heavenly border suffering eternally for a sinful life. In neither of these scenarios does the prospect of the departed being able to, or even wanting to communicate with those left behind, cross our minds. As far as we're concerned, they are gone, never to be seen or heard from again. And for that we grieve.

Admittedly there are others willing to entertain the notion of contact from the departed. However, they assume that should it happen it would be a capital B "Big Deal," and unmistakable. For example, angelic choirs, a clap of thunder, perhaps a streak or two of lightning, or booming voices. We're talking miracles here so it would have to be something remarkable, right? And that's part of the problem. Eight out of ten times after-death communication is so subtle that we dismiss it as one of those things we simply can't explain. Coincidental. Inexplicable. A mystery. Or if we want to impress ourselves with our command of the language, synchronicity. In truth, it's all of that. And more.

Ever been thinking of that old college friend now deceased, who fit the definition of BFF these days? Or your mom or dad, their memory popping up in a moment of sorely missing them? You start your car, the radio blares to life, and the song playing is one of your parent's absolute favorites? You think that's a coincidence? Think again!

Or, as in my case, when April 23 rolls around, I remember being awakened at six in the morning with the call from the nurse's station of the rehab facility telling me that my husband "had coded" and had been rushed to the emergency room with CPR in progress. It wasn't successful and I never got to say good-bye. And in that moment every April 23, I miss him terribly. Immediately, no matter where I am, I briefly detect the scent of his cologne. Then it's gone. But it's a gentle, comforting caress from him. I admit that over the fourteen years he's been gone there has been an April 23rd or two when I forgot. But whenever I haven't, I've gotten that "hello" from Bob.

Oftentimes, that's the way it works. Something simple that reminds you of that person, such as their name on the side of a plumbing truck two seconds after you thought of them. Or a dream in which they appeared, so vivid its impact never leaves us. Contact from our family and friends can occasionally be defined as spectacular—a sighting, hearing their voice, even receiving a message that could only have come from that one person. Those are not everyday occurrences. Yet, they do happen. Far more often, it's simple, subtle, yet undeniable.

He Blew Her a Kiss should be a primer on the subject. Had I been fortunate enough to have read it when my husband began his two-year attempt to make me realize he still existed, I'd have gotten the point far sooner and would have a thousand less gray hairs. This book is a treasure, one that leaves the reader filled with wonder and a warm heart. It opens the mind to possibilities we've never considered and a willingness to greet the next "inexplicable" with a different attitude.

It's a wonderful book. Enjoy.

Chassie West
Author of *No Reasons for Goodbyes*
www.chassiewest.com

Introduction

A joyful day has arrived and we are so happy to present Volume 2 in the *He Blew Her a Kiss* series. This has been a wonderful fulfilling experience for us. Here's a brief retelling of how this journey began in case you weren't fortunate enough to read the first book.

An extremely dear friend of mine, Tom, struggled through the pain of losing his wife, Judy, to cancer. He was definitely in a painful place missing her incredibly, so he decided to send her a love note. He penned his words on the streamers attached to a birthday balloon he had just received. He said a brief prayer. Then, Tom released the balloon into the air and blew her a kiss, all so lovingly.

The next day that very same balloon was sitting right outside his door when he arrived to work. He immediately believed this was "returned" communication from heaven sent by his wife. This single experience was a revelation to Tom. Judy had not left him. She had merely transformed. He knew in his heart that her spirit was close at hand, bringing him great comfort and joy. Tom, like many others, found reassurance that our loved ones don't cease to exist. They simply transition into a more peaceful and spiritual existence. His profound experience, combined with one of my own where my mother came to me after passing, has brought me a passionate desire to help others heal from the loss of a loved one.

Throughout the past few years, we have discovered these types of experiences are called *after-death communication*, and have observed the incredible impact upon their recipients. Bill Guggenheim and his former wife, Judy, coined the term *after-death communication*, or ADC, after conducting many years of research. The couple dedicated an enormous amount of time and love validating the different types of communication they discovered people were experiencing. They were, indeed, pioneers. Like many venturing into the unknown, they gathered a great deal of information. Their efforts helped people understand how our loved ones can communicate with us once they are gone from the physical world. One key fact they revealed is that after-death communication is experienced by people throughout the world who walk different lives, practice different customs, and hold different religious beliefs.

My coauthor, Kelley Dollar, and I also have had the opportunity to speak with hundreds of people about their very own ADC and discovered many of them struggle with two specific emotions. The first emotion, and probably the very first thought for many outsiders, is that the recipient is going crazy. But once the person experiencing the ADC finds the ability to accept it for just what it is, the next trouble appearing in their life is an inability to share it with others. After all, the prospect of being ridiculed is an all-too-human fear.

In spite of this fear of ridicule, many express the healing benefits these ADCs have provided. Sharing their stories not only brought them comfort, it served as a bridge to understanding life after death. Validation of a loved one's well-being vastly accelerated the ability to cope with the loss through grief counseling and other methods. Incidentally, we refer to our collection as a "support group of stories." People bond through association, and relating to others can bring comfort that otherwise might be fairly elusive.

This highly spiritual experience of an ADC is one we believe should be welcomed and thoroughly embraced, never feared. Yes, there are doubters. There will always be someone who questions the validity of an ADC, dismissing it as quite unreal or coincidental and possibly the result of an overly productive imagination.

We know better.

Research has led us to believe our loved ones will often communicate in a manner that is easily recognizable to us, but not necessarily anyone else. The communication holds a special meaning for the recipient. It is personal. It's something that allows for easy recognition of the sender.

It touches the heart.

The most common ADC is referred to as a "sleep-state visit," which many acknowledge as a dream. The message often relayed is "I'm okay and you're going to be fine." This is what I received from my mother after her passing in 1995. This simple message conveys that our loved ones continue to exist in their true spiritual self, quite aware of what's going on around us. They have a desire to let us know they are near, sending us these and other unique messages encouraging us to move forward with our lives.

We chose a different approach to writing our books. Typically, ADC accounts shared are written in first person. There is absolutely nothing wrong with this particular use of first person voice. We decided to write in third person, giving us as writers the opportunity to expand upon personality, backgrounds, and relationships between all parties involved. This provides a true story "feel," making it quite easy to read while still maintaining the integrity of the ADC experience.

Response from the first book has been nothing short of wonderful. Readers have expressed finding joyful peace and healing comfort. Many have shared that our true story presentations have assisted them in transitioning from grief to a more positive outlook on life after death. This reaffirms our desire and goal to share with multitudes of people the beauty and joy that can be realized even in times of fear, sadness, and despair.

Readers of the first book should be quite familiar with Tom and Judy's story, which is the original *He Blew Her a Kiss*. Their story will be included at the beginning of each book in the series so any new reader will gain an understanding of what inspiration lay behind the title and subsequent volumes. Our sincere hope is that you will enjoy every story as much as we have enjoyed sharing them with you. Our intent has always been helping people experiencing a loss find a certain sense of peace. We believe reading the accounts of other people, similar to your own, is an important part of the healing process and one that is extremely beneficial. What is experienced in the middle of painful grief may, in fact, be a beautifully joyful encounter with your loved one in spirit form. We all go through the natural process of pain and grieving.

However, we also can take great comfort knowing one day we will be reunited.

Ultimately, the message we would share through these books is that death is only the physical end. We all know the loss of a loved one is painful for people left behind. Yet, this is nothing but a transition, taking loved ones back to the true spiritual self, free from pain and affliction. Physical bonds are broken but love shared is always eternal. With your support, we are capable of presenting genuine accounts that have, indeed, touched many hearts including ours.

Please consider sharing your story on our website, www.HeBlewHerAKiss.com, and possibly for our next publication. Keep in mind, your experience may be the very bridge in helping others obtain some peaceful perspective concerning what happens when a loved one departs this physical world.

Much love and many blessings,

Angie Pechak Printup
Founder and coauthor, *He Blew Her a Kiss*

He Blew Her a Kiss

The entire *He Blew Her a Kiss* concept can be credited to the following story, which will appear in every book of the series. We consider it to be our signature story.

He Blew Her a Kiss

Tom and Judy were high-school sweethearts living in a small town in Mississippi when they met in the seventh grade. He was so smitten he asked her to sit with him during a movie after a 4H-club event. To his extreme disappointment, she told him no. It was love at first sight for Tom, but his shyness prevented him from pursuing the love of his life again until the eleventh grade. It was then that he worked up the courage to ask Judy out again. This time she said yes, and from that point on they were committed to each other for life. They graduated from high school and, while attending college, decided they couldn't wait any longer, so in 1967 they said their marriage vows and became husband and wife.

After the pair completed their college education, Tom

joined the air force, and they moved to Alaska. In 1972, he fulfilled his obligations to his country and left the service. Together, Tom and Judy moved to a city not far from their hometown. Tom began his career in the banking business and Judy started teaching. Their small family grew to include two children, a boy and a girl.

After spending many years in the city, Tom had the opportunity to become the bank president back in the town where he and Judy grew up. Although they loved their city life and all the friendships they had cultivated, the kids had ventured out on their own, and the couple felt in their hearts this was the right move for them. So, in 1999 Tom accepted the job. Judy had to stay in the city until they could sell their house. It was in this transitional period, during a routine mammogram, that Judy discovered a mass in her breast. It was indeed breast cancer, and in an effort to rid it from her body she underwent a mastectomy in July 1999. After chemo, it was believed she had gone into remission.

For eight years, she faithfully went in for her yearly checkup and, happily, she was always cancer free. However, in the ninth year after her original battle with cancer started, she began experiencing problems in her leg. Sadly, the cancer was back, and this time the invasive predator had moved into her bones, liver, and lungs. She underwent the insufferable sessions of chemo once again, but the disease had gotten too advanced for the treatments to help. On Oct. 12, 2008, Judy's battle with cancer ended, and Tom lost his high-school sweetheart, love of his life, and best friend of 41 years. Or, so he thought...

Tom found himself alone in his house experiencing a loss he could never fully convey to anyone else. How can you possibly function when you become so separated from your soul mate?

Shortly after Judy's passing, Tom received a birthday gift from two of his relatives. It was a beautiful pail of candy, holding down a large happy-birthday balloon with ribbons tied to it. He set the arrangement on the table with no realization this would be the vessel for his communication with his beloved Judy.

A day or so later Tom returned home from work. Rain had settled on their town for the entire day, and it seemed as if nature itself was feeling just as melancholy as he was. Thinking about Judy, his glance fell on the arrangement sitting on the table. It was as if something had compelled him to look that way. Then it hit him. He was going to send his wife a message! Tom excitedly wrote his note on the ribbons, *To Judy, I love you soooooooooooo much, Love Tom*. He then turned it over and addressed it, *This is for you, Judy, in Heaven*.

Tom walked outside and looked around at the tall, majestic trees in front of their house. He dropped his head,

♥ He Blew Her a Kiss

said a little prayer, and then lovingly released the balloon into the air. He blew her a kiss and said, "Judy, here it comes." Tom watched it float ever higher in the gentle wind until it danced up into the clouds and disappeared from sight. Satisfied with his gesture of love, he went back into the house and settled down for the evening.

The next day Tom went through his familiar routine upon arriving at work. As he drove into the parking lot, he scanned around the building to make sure everything appeared as normal. Something caught his eye. He stopped the car and got out. Curious, Tom approached the walkway leading to the door of the bank. His breath stopped in his chest and his heart began beating rapidly. There on the sidewalk was the balloon he had sent to Judy. Although it was deflated, it was otherwise in perfect condition. Lying next to it was the ribbon he had so lovingly written the note upon. Comfort, love, and assurance washed through him because he knew beyond a shadow of a doubt his prayer had been answered and Judy had received his message. It was Judy's way of telling him everything was all right and he didn't have to be sad any longer. She was still with him. He immediately told his coworkers and even called Judy's former coworkers to relate the story to them. Everyone cried tears of joy that day to celebrate Tom and Judy's undying love for one another.

He Blew Her a Kiss ♥

Tom cherished his beloved balloon. He had it framed and proudly displayed in their home. It now served two purposes. First, it became a symbol to him of their love and, second, it afforded him the opportunity to share his story with others. Tom experienced how love transcends all when he sent his wife a love note, riding on the prayer and kiss that he blew to her.

A side note to readers:
Since the inception of this project Tom unexpectedly passed in May 2009, six months after Judy. It has been a heartfelt loss to his family and friends alike. Perhaps God in his infinite mercy spared him further sorrow from a broken heart and reunited him with his beloved Judy. They would have celebrated their 42nd anniversary on June 6, 2009.

Inspirational Stories

For a great majority, all it takes is one firsthand experience to completely convert personal beliefs. That one encounter can lift a person beyond the pain of loss and entirely change their perception of life…and death. A sign, whether subtle or dramatic, provides peace, comfort, relief, and encouragement during a time when it is so desperately needed. The following stories all come from recipients of a single ADC and represent a variety of the 12 most common signs. Each story is a true account and it is our hope that as you read these intimate and personal moments, you will form your own opinions regarding life after death.

A Nugget of Reassurance

For a young and impressionable girl, being in love is a wonderful and exciting place to be. Without a care in the world, they believe with all their heart that nothing can bring them down. Too many times teenagers, being in that euphoric state of mind, build themselves up for major letdowns and disappointments. Lori's first love proved to be her first true heartbreak as well. His lack of interest after learning about her pregnancy did not, however, prevent his parents from becoming involved. They embraced Lori and ultimately Jeffrey with complete love. Even her mother, although not very happy about the circumstances at the time, compassionately stood by her side giving her the love, support, and courage to face the challenges ahead.

♥ He Blew Her a Kiss

On April 24, 1993, Lori gave birth to a beautiful little boy she named Jeffrey William. He was a sweet innocent child that brought great joy to her life and many others. He became her world. She would take him on outings, particularly the park, where he loved to watch the ducks play. While she held him in her arms, he would consistently tug and play with her rings. Children love shiny little objects, and he was especially fond of her gold nugget ring. With inquisitive eyes, Jeffrey studied the prize intently. He would then grasp it with his tiny little fingers, lingering to feel the rough bumpy surface. Lori would gaze lovingly at him, thankful for this precious little one's presence in her life.

Before Lori knew it, an entire year had passed and they celebrated Jeffrey's first birthday. He had lots of new toys to play with, but Lori noticed none held his attention like her gold nugget ring. She had lost the ring at some point, most likely with Jeffrey's help, and missed having his little fingers exploring every facet of it. She quickly brushed those thoughts out of her head and turned her attention back to her little boy. He had grown so much from the time she had brought him home to her mother's house from the hospital. That little bundle had brought so much joy to their hearts they just couldn't imagine what it would be like without looking into his big brown eyes and seeing that adoring smile on his face. Being a single

A Nugget of Reassurance ♥

mother wasn't easy, but the love she saw reflected in his eyes made everything worthwhile.

Just a little over three months after Jeffrey's first birthday on July 31, 1994, Lori endured a tragedy that would forever be imprinted in her mind. Her precious little boy died from an accident. Although they fought furiously to save his life, nothing could be done. At the time, she and Jeffrey were living with a friend, and as soon as her mother received the news she came immediately to comfort her beloved daughter. Instinctively, her mother packed Lori's belongings and took her straight home with her. She knew how difficult this was going to be for her daughter to overcome.

The pain and numbness seemed to take up residence in Lori's life. Refusing to eat she continued to withdraw, preferring to sit alone in her room staring at the walls. Despite her mother and stepfather's attempts to lift her spirits, Lori had to deal with the loss in her own way and in her own time. Eventually she made the effort to get out of the house. Without any destination in mind she just started driving. So many memories were flooding her thoughts when all of a sudden she heard the siren of an ambulance. She swerved, nearly running off the road to move out of the way. Then she realized there was no ambulance. Her mind began to race. If people had moved out of the way quicker maybe the ambulance could have

♥ He Blew Her a Kiss

gotten to her son sooner! She so desperately wanted to be able to blame this senseless loss on someone, on something. Looking in the rear-view mirror she saw the empty car seat still strapped in the backseat and the tears fell relentlessly down her cheeks.

Lori's mother immediately decided it was best to eliminate some of the painful reminders of Jeffrey's absence. The car seat, his crib, and other items were removed in an attempt to help her move forward with life. Her mother even bought Lori a new car for her birthday in September. With the help of friends, she began trying to put the pieces of her life back in order. She started going out and spending time with other people, and little by little things slowly got better. One evening she was out with a girlfriend and became engaged in a conversation with her friend's boyfriend. Lori noticed he wore a gold nugget ring. She asked if she could see it. As she held it in her hand, tears began to trickle down her face. A little later she decided it was time to head home.

It was quite a long drive to her mother's house since they lived out in the country in what seemed to be the middle of nowhere. The time alone allowed her to reflect upon memories the nugget ring had brought to the forefront. She turned onto the gravel driveway and pulled up to the house. Lori remained seated in the car as the tears welled up. She terribly regretted the loss of the ring

A Nugget of Reassurance ♥

her son had loved so much. She longed to be able to see her son one more time or, at the very least, have a sign that he was all right. After the tears finally subsided, she attempted to compose herself in case her mother was still up. She did not want her mother to know she had been crying again. Lori opened up the door and turned sideways to exit the car. As her feet touched the ground, she leaned forward and something caught her eye. She thought she saw the light from the porch reflect off of something. Reaching down she grasped the object, and much to her amazement realized it was the gold nugget ring she had lost. She tried to reason with herself about how it could have gotten there and that it just wasn't possible. She had moved twice since it disappeared, so it couldn't possibly have found its way to the middle of the countryside and end up in her mother's driveway. With no other apparent explanation, she knew it had to be the sign she had begged for. She turned her eyes up to the stars and smiled.

Lori was so incredibly thankful for that little nugget of reassurance for which her heart and soul craved. For the first time since her son had passed away, she felt a smile adorning her face. A sense of peace slowly spread through her soul, giving her the courage necessary to finally release the hurt and pain that had held her tightly in its grip. Moving forward would be difficult and full of ups

♥ He Blew Her a Kiss

and downs, but Lori gained great comfort in the belief that Jeffrey was in a wonderful place and one day she would look into his big brown eyes again.

~ Submitted by Lori Wallace

Remembering Ma

Jack sat on the front porch of his grandparents' old home place, exhausted from a day of cleaning and packing. The sad responsibility of removing a lifetime of possessions had fallen upon him. However, he felt it was a privilege to say good-bye to a time, a place, and two people whom he loved with all his heart and who loved and cared so deeply for him.

The house behind him was dark and empty now but in his mind's eye, and in the secret places of his heart, it would always remain lit and alive with precious memories and tender mercies. This was the place where he always felt safe and secure. It would forever be a place where love lived, the place that made him who he was.

In the quietness of the moment, and washed in tears,

♥ He Blew Her a Kiss

he replayed scenes from his childhood now lost to time and maturity:

- The faint echoes of children at play; the whack of a Wiffle ball hitting a plastic bat; the children's cries of "You're it!"
- Big, sweet juicy watermelons accompanied by seed-spitting contests "Mater' samitches" with tomato slices so big they would hang out the sides of the bread
- A simmering pot of chicken 'n' dumplings on the stove with his beloved Ma tending the pot
- The wooden mop handle which transformed into a white horse and a hearty "Hi-ho Silver away!"
- Endless summers of swimming, skating, cane poles, cherry popsicles, and vacation Bible school
- Nap time with the sound of the black metal oscillating fan lulling children to sleep

Jack's memories of endless summers and all the wonderful activities were happy ones, but his most cherished memories involved Ma with her gentle and unconditional love. Favorite times included being covered in blankets in the back room, dabbed with Vick's Vapor Rub on his chest and under his nose by Ma's gentle hands; the afterglow of a hot bath followed by a good dousing of Ma's favorite

Remembering Ma ♥

bath-and-body powder and ultimately being wrapped up Indian-style in a fluffy towel, kissed, hugged, and finally lugged off to bed.

This house indeed held a lifetime of memories, and saying good-bye was like losing a best friend. It had been difficult when his grandfather passed, but now that Ma was gone the house that held so much love seemed empty and alone.

A familiar sight broke into his reverie as he gazed upon the creeping shadows of the evening. Tiny dots of glowing yellow light flickered on and off in the field. Jack recalled the excitement had by all when, as children, they would run around strategically capturing the dancing lights in Mason jars. They would laugh and swell with pride as the warm glow of the fireflies multiplied within their jar. It all seemed so long ago.

A sudden sadness washed over Jack as the reason for being there came back to mind. After 80 years of life, Ma's body and mind had slowly begun to betray her. By the time she turned 84, she was confined to a hospital bed being cared for by her daughter, Jack's favorite aunt. It was Christmastime, and Jack and his family made the trip from Texas back to his grandparents' home in Mississippi. His first stop was to immediately visit Ma at the hospital.

Jack walked into the room and love filled his heart as he saw Ma. Her frail, white-headed body was curled

♥ He Blew Her a Kiss

up like a baby. He gently touched her shoulder and she opened her blue eyes, once bright and sparkling but now dimmed by disease. She smiled at his greeting and he softly said, "I love you, Ma," just as he always did. Of course she replied back as she always had with, "I love you, Son." They shared a bond that neither age, separation, or illness would ever break.

As his family left the hospital room, his aunt pulled him to the side to inform him the doctor felt she would not last much longer. For the remainder of their time back in Mississippi, Jack visited Ma every day. Finally it was time to return home, so with hugs and kisses he left Ma with the promise of seeing her in the spring.

Jack and his family returned to Texas and quickly got back into the routine of working all day and then watching the kids play basketball. In mid-January, it seemed as if the Arctic Express had rushed in from the North Pole, bringing the frigid winds with it. The weather turned bitterly cold and the skies a dull gray. Jack's day at the Kroger Distribution Center had been long and hard. He longed to get home to a meal, a bath, and some relaxation time in his comfortable blue chair. What he wanted and what he got were not what he expected. Not even close.

As soon as Jack walked through the door, his senses were overwhelmed by the smell of Vick's Vapor Rub. The nostalgic, comforting aroma filled the entire house. His

Remembering Ma ♥

wife had put some Vick's Vapor Steam on the stovetop because one of the kids had a cold. He shared with her how it brought back wonderful memories of Ma and her house. At that moment, he felt better than he had the entire day.

Sherry, his wife of 20 years, had drawn a bath for him and told him to hurry up because they were going to have a surprise supper. Most of the time he understood that to be code for "I'm not cooking tonight…what kind of pizza do you want delivered?" However, this wasn't like most of the time. Sherry informed him that their neighbor Marti had called and wanted to bring them supper that night. It was a "thank you" for all the yard work Jack and his family had done for her the previous summer and fall. Marti had been widowed and Jack believed that his family should help out because that is what the Good Book instructed. It states in James 1:27, "Religion that God our Father accepts as pure and faultless is this: to look after orphans and widows…," and also in Luke 10:25-37, "Who was the neighbor? The one who showed mercy, go and do likewise." It was something he needed no thanks for doing but he appreciated her kind offering.

Jack was firmly embedded in his La-Z-Boy when the doorbell rang. He opened the door and there stood his neighbor Marti with an enormous pot of chicken and dumplings! She cheerfully said, "Sherry told me how much you loved chicken and dumplings and that your

♥ He Blew Her a Kiss

grandmother used to make them especially for you. These may not be as good as hers but they were made especially for you." Jack thanked her profusely and thought to himself, this is turning into a great day!

After stuffing himself with chicken and dumplings, which weren't the same as Ma's but a real close second, he made his way back to his chair, this time with pen and paper. He proceeded to write Ma a letter to tell her about his day and to once again thank her for all the love she had given him. It was a lot of love, too, because he had spent so much time with her growing up. It was by far his favorite place to be, hands down.

The phone rang just as he finished. Sherry answered it and listened intently. She then handed Jack the phone and told him it was his Aunt Nancy. Jack knew immediately in his heart what the call was about. His aunt softly repeated herself, "Ma died about two hours ago. She was in no pain. She just stopped breathing." They talked for a few more minutes about the family and the funeral. After saying "I love you" and "good-bye," Jack hung up the phone and went to the bedroom and closed the door.

Jack expressed the deep penetrating pain in his heart with suffocating sobs. The separation and loss he felt came from the very depths of his soul. His grandmother had meant the world to him, and he couldn't imagine a life without her presence in it. It is necessary to accept mortality for it is a natural process. Nevertheless, it is painful for people left behind. He knew he had to dry the tears for there were matters that had to be attended to. The family packed up and loaded into the car. In the wee hours of the morning they left for Mississippi just ahead of yet another winter storm.

The funeral was a time to say good-bye to their beloved Ma. But, it was also a time of remembrance to celebrate the life and love of a woman that meant so much to them all. It was a comfort to hear the minister say, "Blessed in the sight of the Lord is the death of one of his saints," and to know that Ma heard those loving words, "Well done thy good and faithful servant." Through it all Jack also could look forward to the joyous reunion that would one day come.

After his emotions calmed down, Jack realized God in His infinite grace had allowed Ma, even from miles away, to say good-bye to her loving grandson. It came by way of the familiar scent of Vick's Vapor Rub and the simmering pot of chicken and dumplings that transported his soul back to a time of joy and unconditional love. It was his grandmother's way of confirming her love for him. But, it served even more to affirm the abundant love the Heavenly Father had for both of them. Jack is thankful every day for the simple yet powerful message he received from his beloved Ma.

~ Submitted by Jack C. "Chuck" Provine

In the Line of Duty

In spite of the incredible physical pain that can accompany childbirth, Debra rejoiced as the doctor introduced her beautiful baby boy. A bundle of 10 pounds, 11 ounces, her son Cole was the most beautiful baby on earth. There was no way to express the love that permeated every ounce of her being. Nothing else in the world mattered.

It was with great pride and joy Debra brought her newborn home. With loving and devoted attentiveness, she cared for him. She nurtured him and watched him grow, amazed and elated every step of the way. Mentally checking off each milestone he achieved filled her heart with pride.

With each passing year, Debra felt completely blessed to have such a wonderful son. He was active, athletic,

♥ He Blew Her a Kiss

and very driven. When Cole set his mind to it, he could accomplish anything. That driving determination served him well growing up. He modeled himself after his father, who had made a career as a highway trooper. The dedication his father had for his job instilled in Cole a certain passion to follow in his father's footsteps. Debra cringed at the thought, however. She was much too aware of the dangers involved in being a police officer. The thought of her son being in harm's way scared her more than she wanted to admit.

Cole had become a strapping young man by the time he graduated. He stood a full 6 ft. 5 in. He was in perfect shape and determined to join the force. He longed for his mother's approval but she just couldn't provide it. The fear of losing her only child was too much to overcome. Despite her misgivings, he pursued his dream and applied to the police department.

It had been seven months since Cole completed his mandated training. His success was no surprise to his mother, for she had watched him accomplish goals his entire life. One morning they stood in her kitchen discussing his new career. With a heartfelt plea, she asked him, "What if something happens to you?" Cole smiled at his mother, attempting to reassure her, and said in his most sincere tone, "Momma, I love this job. I have never been happier." Then she heard the words that would stay with her forever. Cole simply stated, "I would rather have 20 minutes of happiness than a lifetime of nothing."

Debra knew her son loved his job. He was perfectly suited to be in a life of service to others. Cole was a caring, compassionate soul that loved to help others. He was one of the fortunate ones that realize their passion as a young child and grow up to fulfill it. He felt an immense satisfaction and peace in that accomplishment.

Only two weeks later, Debra jumped out of a deep sleep as the phone rang at two o'clock in the morning. Fear leapt into her heart as she reached for it. She knew nothing good would come at this time of the morning. While driving to the hospital, her mind raced. All she had been told was there had been an accident. Her husband drove the car as quickly as possible. They ran into the emergency room urgently calling, "Where is Cole?" She stopped dead in her tracks as a group came forward with solemn looks on their faces. Everyone seemed to be moving in slow motion. As soon as they uttered the words, "I'm sorry," Debra felt her legs give out from underneath her and she crumpled to the floor. She screamed out, "No, please God, not Cole!"

What Debra had feared most in her life reared its ugly head as if mocking her. What would she do? She couldn't imagine a world without Cole. Despair raced in and she believed in that moment she would rather end her life

♥ He Blew Her a Kiss

than go on without her son. Her husband gathered her up, trying everything to console her but to no avail. The next thing she remembered was being at the house. Her mind fought to clear the fog that had taken over. Somehow, together, they made arrangements for their son.

The night before the funeral Debra had finally succumbed to sleep. Suddenly, Cole was there. He was in the new car he had purchased only a few weeks earlier. He had on one of his favorite shirts and a leather coat. It was so real. She noticed all the vivid details. Then she heard him speak, "Momma, I have to go now." Debra asked him if it was very different. He replied, "It's not too different but I have to go." She told her son how very much she loved him and then as quickly as he appeared, he was gone.

Debra had that dream more than seven years ago and can still see it as clearly as she did that night. She was fully convinced her son, knowing her fears, had made sure to come and say his last good-bye. That brief encounter brought her great comfort and the very strength she needed to make it through the funeral.

As time has slowly passed Debra still feels the void in her heart, and there isn't a day that goes by that she doesn't think of Cole. She often sees dragonflies, which she feels he has sent, particularly when she is having a difficult day. Her heart fills with his love and the incredible sensation that he is telling her, "Momma, don't cry. I am here." How appropriate that Cole would choose a dragonfly to send to his mother because, interestingly enough, the dragonfly symbolizes many things. They represent change, living each moment to the fullest, and self-realization. These signs or communications from her son are experiences she cherishes and draws upon in the daily recovery process for losing a child. Knowing her son is near gives her added strength needed to move forward with her life, conquering it one day at a time.

~ Submitted by Debra Hickman

Morning Glory! Rise and Shine

Marriage is not only the joining of two people in matrimony, but it is a merging of two families as well. Debbie considered herself extremely fortunate to acquire Aletha Green as her mother-in-law. She dearly loved and respected her as much as her own mother. So often in-laws can cause newlyweds unnecessary strife within their relationship, but it was not so in this case. Aletha was warm and caring and let it be known how much she adored her new daughter-in-law.

Debbie and her husband married in 1982. After about eight years of marriage, they welcomed their new son Chris into the world. Of course, he was the apple of everyone's eye. Aletha spoiled him as all grandparents tend to do. She

♥ He Blew Her a Kiss

made sure it was always a happy time when they came to visit. Her favorite way to wake them up in the mornings was to cheerfully call out, "Morning Glory...rise and shine!" Her happy little greeting stemmed from her love for morning glories. A unique feature of the flower is that in the spring they bloom every morning as the sun creeps up in the sky and it withers away at the end of each day.

Aletha met each day with a smile on her face just like her morning glories. She had a kindness about her that just radiated out to those around her. Her optimism and love was inspiring. It was because of her outgoing, happy personality the news of cancer was so heartbreaking.

In 1996, Aletha was diagnosed with stage 4 breast cancer. It was difficult for everyone that knew her to see such a kind and loving woman going through the pain of this crippling disease. Within two years, the cancer had spread to her bones, liver, and brain. Sadly she passed away in August 1998. The loss of Aletha added to the marital strains Debbie and her husband had been going through. Only a month later, he filed for a divorce.

Debbie had been so close to Aletha, she felt as though she had lost her own mother. Putting the divorce into the mix only added to an already painful situation. They decided to sell their house and Debbie and Chris moved out on their own. She bought a brand new patio home in March 1999. As springtime descended upon them, much to her surprise,

Morning Glory! Rise and Shine ♥

there were morning glories sprouting out from her front flowerbed. She was astonished because no one had lived in this house before her and there had been no mention of anyone planting these flowers. Debbie felt sure Aletha was letting her know that no matter what, she still loved them very much and was watching over them. This gave Debbie much needed comfort after some very trying times.

Two years later, in the spring of 2001, Debbie remarried. She and her husband decided to move about two miles from where she currently lived. After they had been at the new house approximately a month, she was in the backyard and was thrilled to see morning glories growing on the back fence. Neither she nor her husband had planted them. It was as if they'd materialized on their own. Debbie knew in her heart no matter where she was, she was loved and looked after by Aletha. Chris was only eight-years-old when his grandmother passed away, but he remembers the morning glories growing in her yard and how much they meant to her. He, too, felt like she was letting them know how much she loved them. Just like the morning glories face each day happy and secure in the warmth of the sun, Debbie and Chris could face each day embracing the love Aletha so deeply felt for them, secure in the belief she was never far away.

~ Submitted by Debbie White

A Name Says It All

Every day we make choices in our lives. We choose what kind of career we want, where we live, and even the friends we keep. We don't necessarily choose with whom we fall in love. A combination of events can sometimes lead us to the one we are meant to be with, however, we have no control over the circumstances. When Lisa found the man she wanted to spend the rest of her life with, he came as a package deal. Tim already had a 14-year-old son, Josh, from a previous relationship. Becoming a stepfather or stepmother can sometimes be quite challenging. It is only natural there will be conflicts and personality clashes until you reach a balance. In order to achieve that balance, there has to be a great deal of love, patience, flexibility, and respect for one another.

♥ He Blew Her a Kiss

In Lisa's case, she was lucky. It only took a few times of butting heads to begin developing their own unique relationship. Josh, or JT as they called him, was a great kid. He accepted Lisa and learned over time to respect and even value her opinions. It is never an easy task to take on the role of a parent with someone else's child, but Lisa loved Tim and grew to love his son Josh with an equal amount of devotion.

JT was your typical teenager—intelligent, but with other things on his mind besides schoolwork. It is frustrating to see your child who you know has potential, but fails to apply it. At one point he was part of a band. This was no surprise considering how much he loved music. But where he really shined was with writing. He was very artistic and creative, dreaming of becoming a songwriter. He kept a journal and continued nurturing his dream. In spite of his obvious intelligence, JT ended up making decisions that were detrimental not only to himself, but to his dreams as well.

Some acquaintances can be very destructive, and choosing the wrong crowd can lead to a great deal of heartache and misery. JT experienced much of this, and by his mid-20s it was determined that leaving the neighborhood and city he grew up in would be in his best interest. He decided to move to Denver, where his mother Bev had lived since he was 15. The general thinking was that with a fresh city he could obtain a fresh start.

A Name Says It All ♥

After JT arrived in Denver, he met a young lady named Jesi with whom he began to have a serious relationship. Things were looking much brighter for his future. He enrolled in college to get a degree and worked at a full-time job. For once, it seemed as though he was on a better path. Jesi soon revealed to him that he was going to be a father. He was determined to be a wonderful father and loving partner to Jesi. They had a beautiful baby girl they named Paige. She was adored by everyone and, for the first two years of her life, JT did just as he had promised himself. He stayed on the straight and narrow and provided for them as best as he knew how.

Old demons are hard to escape, though, and eventually they caught up with him. Their deceptive and destructive thoughts began to persevere in his mind, bringing about a change in him his soul truly did not want. He tried to resist, but unfortunately the path he took led directly to a tragic ending for all.

Lisa and Tim had been hanging on to the hopes that JT had finally turned his life around for the better. He had a beautiful little girl to serve as inspiration and motivation, and they truly felt everything was going to be okay. At least that's what they dreamed of until April 2008, when they received that devastating call which seems to suck the very life from your body. JT was gone and there was nothing they could do to help him. With despair and helplessness,

♥ He Blew Her a Kiss

they immediately boarded a plane for Denver to see their son one last time. The service was quite emotional for everyone attending. All the family members knew what a struggle it had been for JT, and yet they were filled with frustration for what his life could have been. Seeing Paige, so young and innocent, left without a father to watch her grow up, only added to their pain. The road ahead would be difficult, but for Paige's sake the family would have to be strong in order to provide her all the love and support that she would most assuredly need.

A few months after JT's passing, Tim still battled with the loss of his only son. Determined to help him through such a difficult stage, Lisa felt it was important they engage in some activity together. She decided to enroll them in a welding class. Even though she knew absolutely nothing about welding, she thought it was something that would keep them busy. It would also be good they could do it together. At times of a loss such as a child, no matter the age, parents sometimes drift apart in the grieving process. This is not an intentional separation. It is just that each person deals with grief in different ways. Lisa believed participating together would help strengthen their bond even more, and in turn help each other through such a heartbreaking transition.

To Lisa's amazement, Tim agreed. She worried initially he would reject the idea because the class would be held

A Name Says It All ♥

at JT's old high school. She was a little concerned it might bring up painful memories, but Tim was all for trying something new. They went to the very first class and had the opportunity to meet other students and the instructor. He turned out to be a wonderful man and, as he shared a little of his life and background with the class, they learned he had two sons of his own. After the instructor taught them some of the basics, he then paired everyone off. Of course, Lisa and Tim were paired together as they proceeded to one of the welding stations. They ended up with the last one on the far side of the room. As they approached, they saw a welded cutout standing proudly at their station. They were a little shocked and caught off-guard as they read it. It simply said, "JOSHUA." Their hearts jumped up in their throats for a moment just seeing their son's name. The instructor, observing their reaction, came to investigate what was going on. Scratching his head, he explained that each student was required to clean up their area every day. The most unusual fact he revealed was that not one of his students was named Joshua.

Lisa and Tim had no doubt in their minds JT had given them a sign. He knew how they were struggling with his loss and he wanted to convey to them he was indeed all right. Not only did he accomplish this with a simple sign, they also believed more importantly he was still a part of their lives and they too would be okay.

♥ He Blew Her a Kiss

The knowledge our loved one is never truly separated from us is a very comforting thought. We only need to adjust our beliefs and adapt to a relationship of completely different dynamics. What a joy it is to know you can speak to your departed loved one at any time, at any place, and believe it is not just words drifting in the air. They hear us, they watch us, and they know what we are going through. We simply have to learn to listen in an entirely new way. As much as a person struck blind has to learn to "see" with their other senses, we have to learn to hear and recognize our loved ones, not only through physical signs, but also from our inner self. For people who have not had the blessed opportunity to communicate with a loved one who has passed, keep your heart and mind open. Ask someone who has and they will tell you what an amazing, healing, and joyful experience it can be. In Tim and Lisa's experience, JT used a simple but effective way to communicate, and for them a single name said it all.

~ Submitted by Lisa Watson

A Saint's Farewell

Having a child is not only a blessing, but it is also a lifetime of lessons. The day they come home from the hospital it begins. Sleepless nights, exhausting hours, and never-ending tasks become the daily routine. But, God in his infinite mercy gave women an immense capacity for love and patience. When you find yourself with that small break in a hectic schedule and you are holding that sweet, helpless child in your arms, it seems to make all the work worthwhile. As they continue to grow up, you praise God each time they complete a phase in their life that leads to their own independence.

There are parents, however, that are not able to rejoice in those evolving milestones. Some parents face caring for a child with a handicap, either mental or physical, and find

♥ He Blew Her a Kiss

the passing of time may not bring about the fulfillment of development. It takes special individuals to conquer such an ultimate test of fortitude and stamina. Geri's ex-mother-in-law, Marie, was one such special individual.

When Marie was 20 years old, she delivered a baby girl that suffered a brain injury during childbirth, leaving her mentally handicapped. Although she had four other children, Marie never shirked her duties as a mother. She devoted her entire life to the care and nurturing of her baby girl that never really grew up. Thankfully, she had her loving husband Domenick by her side providing that little bit of strength she sometimes needed to continue on.

For 64 years, Marie lived the life of a loving mother and wife. She tended her family with the greatest love and attention she possessed, and not once did she ever complain. Geri considered her mother-in-law a saint by the example she set, humbly accepting the life she had been given. Unfortunately, Marie had yet another challenge to endure as God saw fit to take her husband home. After Domenick's passing, as with any couple that had shared so many years together, Marie felt the void he had left in her heart. However, she was not the woman to give up so she persevered in spite of her loss. After all, she still had her daughter to look after.

One day Marie's son Rico and his wife Mollye came to visit. After his father passed, Rico made sure he stopped

A Saint's Farewell ♥

by to check on his mother as often as possible. While sitting in the den, they heard the door open and a shuffling of feet on the floor. They called out, asking who was there but got no response. Then they heard the shuffling again and it struck a familiar chord. Both agreed it sounded just like Domenick when he used to walk through the house. They got up to check and discovered they were the only two in the room. They were amazed yet convinced that it had to be him. There was no other explanation. Rico felt an immediate sense of comfort knowing his father continued to keep an eye on the wife he'd loved for so many years.

As Marie's age progressed, so did the wear and tear on her body. Her knee had gotten so bad doctors recommended a knee replacement. Marie would have nothing to do with that. Her daughter needed her and she could not be out of commission for the time necessary to heal. Her decision was final, and she would just deal with the pain as long as possible. Eventually, both her knees deteriorated to the point she was crippled and unable to see to her daughter's needs. It had been five years since Domenick had died, and her spirit was growing weary. As her appetite began to fade and her soul sensed her husband's presence, she started expressing her readiness to depart this world. She knew he was waiting to guide her home.

♥ He Blew Her a Kiss

One pleasant evening around this time, Geri had been outside and looked up in the sky and saw a gorgeous rainbow stretching across the heavens. The peculiar part was that it had not rained a drop. She immediately flashed back to the last time she had seen a rainbow. It had marked the day her stepmother had passed away seven years earlier. Because of that, Geri intuitively knew her ex-mother-in-law's time was close at hand. The next morning when her daughter Gina called to tell her, she was sad but not surprised to hear Marie had departed. Gina also had to wake her daughter Christina that same morning to give her the news. When Gina woke her to explain Granny Marie had gone to Heaven, Christina cried herself back to sleep and had a magnificent dream.

The next day after Marie's passing, Geri was visiting Gina when her granddaughter Christina approached her and recounted the dream she'd had about her Granny Marie. Christina told Geri that Granny was standing over her, but she looked younger. Granny then leaned over, kissed Christina on the cheek, and told her she loved her and not to worry about her because she was okay. Then Christina revealed something that completely surprised Geri. She said, "Mimi, I always thought angel's wings were white but Granny's were just like two rainbows." Geri thought about the rainbow she had seen but had not mentioned to anyone. Christina's innocent revelation simply confirmed what Geri already believed in her heart. Although she would deeply miss her, Geri found comfort knowing that Marie had returned home. A place where the love she had so freely given would be returned tenfold.

~ Submitted by Geri Maxwell

The Blessing of a Child

For anyone that is a mother, they will attest to the truth that having a child is a privilege God has given us. To be trusted with the task of caring for, and providing love to, our Heavenly Father's precious little angels is a great responsibility. That honor had been bestowed to Ellen twice previously, with this one being her third son, Clay. He was a beautiful baby boy with crystal clear blue eyes, black hair, and incredibly long eyelashes. The older he got, the more it seemed like angels had dotted his cheeks with their kisses. Always with a smile on his face, this little boy loved life and was a joy to be around. Clay had even become big brother to his younger twin siblings. With the innocence of childhood hugging him like a blanket, he was living large in his own little world.

♥ He Blew Her a Kiss

For nine years, Ellen enjoyed watching her son grow and learn. He experienced quite a few things at his young age. Like any other child, Clay developed friendships and once had a play "date" with one of the little girls in the neighborhood. He also experienced a trip to the police station for being in the right place at the wrong time. Then, there was one incident that particularly stuck out in Ellen's mind, proving his heart was full of the love in which we are created. Clay had a wonderful, generous heart and one Christmas, rather than asking for presents like all the other children, he wanted to give some clothes to a couple of friends. He told Ellen, "Mom, I just want to give them some warm clothes instead of getting everything I want." She was completely moved by the compassion her son had displayed and couldn't have been more proud of him.

Early Sunday morning, Jan. 25, 1998, Ellen's family awoke to a brand new day not realizing what it held in store for them. Shortly after the day had begun, it took a turn for the worse and she found herself on the way to the hospital with Clay. Preoccupied outside of the immediate situation, he stared out the window of the car. Very calmly he informed Ellen that he was going to die. Trying to reassure him that everything would be all right, she felt the tears welling up in her eyes.

Ellen sensed Clay was actually seeing his angels

The Blessing of a Child ♥

coming to comfort him in a very desperate and tragic turn of events not long after they arrived at the emergency room. A mere six hours after they had gotten up that morning, she had to say good-bye as her precious son flew on the wings of angels to be with his Creator, the very author of his short, young life. It is only natural to question the timing of when God calls his own home, especially when we feel it is much too soon. Unable to see the big picture, especially right away, we must always rely on the wisdom of God and the fact that each of us has a purpose in life.

After the loss of her son, Ellen grieved, but she also celebrated what time she had been able to spend with Clay. With the entire family feeling the hurt and pain, she knew as a mother she had to be strong. Sticking to her day-to-day routine kept her going, along with taking care of the rest of her children. A mother's work is never done, and staying busy did not leave much time to spend on regrets.

Three years had passed since she said good-bye to her precious son, and Ellen still longed to hear his voice again. It was Mother's Day and as she stood in the shower, the warm water streaming down her back, she desperately tried to explain to her Lord how she felt. She didn't know if she could bear to sit through another Mother's Day Sunday service without Clay by her side. The honor and

♥ He Blew Her a Kiss

recognition of being a mother felt somewhat hollow after her loss. It wasn't that she discredited having her other children there. It was just that she didn't feel complete. For a brief moment, God calmed her sobs and quieted her heart. In that moment of peace, she clearly heard her son's voice as he said to her, "Happy Mother's Day, Mom. I love you." There was no doubt in her mind it was Clay's voice she heard. What an incredible gift she had received that day. Eternally grateful for God's mercy and love, she would cherish that memory for as long as she lived.

Aware of God's love for her, she was thankful and comforted in the knowledge her son was in such loving care until she could be with him again for all eternity. How tender is the love of a mother and how comforting is the love of a son. Our own children are, in essence, on loan to us to raise, nurture, and care for as they begin their life here. Regardless of how long we have them, it is truly an honor to experience the blessing of a child.

~ Submitted by Ellen Gwyn

A Promise Kept

Cancer is a word none of us want to hear, but in reality will probably affect each and every one of us in some way. It can strike anyone at any time and so often the outcome is devastating. Some cancers are treatable through chemotherapy, radiation, and even surgery, while others have a less than promising prognosis. Research has shown the leading cause of cancer deaths among men is lung cancer. There are two main groups of lung cancer: non-small cell, which accounts for about 85 percent, and the less frequent small-cell lung cancer. Due to the aggressive nature of small-cell lung cancer and the failure to catch it in the early stages, it can be the deadliest.

As Gilda and her husband Rodney listened to the doctor explain the cause of Rodney's fatigue, it felt as if all

♥ He Blew Her a Kiss

the air had been sucked out of the room. Diagnosed with small-cell lung cancer, their outlook on life had instantly become dismal with little hope of restoration. Numbness gripped them as they made their way back home. How would they cope with something of such magnitude? The best prognosis the doctor could give him was 6 to 12 months. As with so many others faced with their own mortality, the things they had considered important drastically changed. Time, which is so easily taken for granted, suddenly became very precious to both of them.

Gilda was frightened at the prospect of losing her husband. Ever since they met, they had been inseparable. They were like Frick and Frack, a phrase commonly used for two people who are closely linked. If you saw one of them, the other was most certainly close by. Although she was afraid of what her future would be like, she was determined to be strong and encouraging for Rodney. Gilda spent as much time as possible caring for him and tending to his needs. As the cancer progressed, he experienced difficulty in breathing and had to have the assistance of an oxygen tank. She continued to show him and express to him her unconditional love. During several of their conversations about what was coming, Gilda begged him to please give her a sign to let her know everything was okay. He agreed to her request knowing how much his wife would need the reassurance.

A Promise Kept ♥

On Nov. 24, 2010, Rodney passed away 30 minutes before Thanksgiving Day. It had only been a few weeks earlier they had celebrated their ninth wedding anniversary. When she married Rodney, she had planned to spend the rest of her life with him. She had pictured the both of them together, retired and enjoying the golden years. Life had different plans, and now she found herself having to adjust to being alone. Tears flowed regularly as she mourned his loss. Repeatedly, she would cry out to him asking him to please, please send her a sign. She even reminded him of the promise he had made. She made sure he knew it had to be an unmistakable sign, one she wouldn't be able to explain away. It had been three weeks and she was still waiting for him to let her know everything was okay.

After Rodney's death, there were many legal things for which Gilda had to attend. It seemed like every night after work she was searching through papers for one thing or another. Finally, after looking everywhere for the car title, she remembered one place she had not checked. She went straight to the drawer that contained all her husband's research about his cancer and other assorted medical papers. She situated herself on the floor and went through each piece of paper, sorting and stacking them in front of her. About halfway through her search, she came across a Christmas card and Valentine's Day card. They

♥ He Blew Her a Kiss

were unsigned but had obviously been bought for her in advance by her husband. Tears sprang from her eyes and she broke down into sobs. Her love for him was overwhelming, and such a simple gesture meant the world to her. It was the best Christmas gift and Valentine's gift she could ever imagine receiving now. She looked up towards heaven and said, "Thank you, honey."

Before going to bed that evening, Gilda had decided to return the nightlight that had been removed to accommodate Rodney's oxygen tank. While she was at it, she went ahead and replaced all the nightlight bulbs in the house. Finally, after slipping under the covers, Gilda closed her eyes and fell fast asleep. She slumbered peacefully until around 3 am, when she woke from a dream about Rodney. Sensing a presence she couldn't explain, Gilda made her way into the kitchen for a glass of water.

As she climbed back into bed, the nightlight she had just plugged in earlier went out. Gilda was frustrated because she knew it was a brand new bulb that shouldn't go out. She proceeded to get back up to check on it but, before she could, the light suddenly came back on. Now she wondered if there could be a short in the light. Deciding to wait until morning to check it, she laid back down. The light went out again. After about 30 seconds it came back on. Four times it repeated this little sequence, and she began to think it was a little strange. Gilda got up and again

A Promise Kept ♥

went in the kitchen, a little unnerved by the entire ordeal. After a while, she decided it best to go on to bed because she had an early morning ahead of her.

Just as the new day dawned, so did Gilda's comprehension of the events that had transpired. A newfound excitement sprang up with the realization that her husband had kept his promise. Her weeks of anxiously waiting were over, and at last she believed in her heart that all was well with Rodney. A wave of peaceful comfort swept over her as she turned her eyes upward and thanked her husband once again. Gilda wrapped that reassurance tightly around her heart and faced the future confident Rodney would always be with her, steadfastly watching over her.

Special Note:
Gilda did check the nightlight and found it to be in perfect working order, and since that night it has never gone out again.

~ Submitted by Gilda Proctor

Love Shines Bright

On Sunday, June 27, 2004, Guy and his wife Jo-Anne had spent a lovely morning out to breakfast with family. The day was beautiful as they made their way back to his parents' house. Guy's sister, Ann, had come for a visit from her home in Georgia. Another sister, June, who was unable to join them for breakfast, met them at their parents' to see Ann off. Upon walking in, she commented that she had just heard a cousin of theirs had been killed last night on his ATV at a gathering for a pig roast. Jo-Anne immediately blurted out that their son Billy had gone to a party last night too and he had an ATV as well. As soon as the words came out of her mouth, a panic overcame her. She retrieved her cell phone and attempted to dial his number. Guy and Jo-Anne were so nervous they found it difficult to recall Billy's number. Somehow they remembered the number to her son's best friend and managed to get it dialed. Her heart sank as soon as she heard his voice. She could tell he was emotionally distraught. Right then and there she realized her attempt at reassurance had turned into a dagger of unmerciful pain.

Guy saw his wife's reaction and his world collapsed. The beautiful day they had been enjoying suddenly became gray and ominous. His emotions opened up like a floodgate and triggered his body into action. Desperately trying to escape the truth, he just ran and ran. As fatigue and shock set in, he became aware he was standing in a hallway, trapped. The only thought raging through his mind screamed, how could this have happened? How could his son die before him? It just wasn't supposed to happen that way! Billy had his entire life ahead of him, a future full of opportunities. Why?

Guy began shutting down as the family attempted to gather themselves. There were things that had to be addressed and things that needed to be handled. It was Jo-Anne's strength that propelled them forward. In a state of confusion, they drove to the fire department. A cousin worked there and it was imperative they have confirmation of what their hearts already knew. On the way, Jo-Anne's thoughts went to their other son Bobby. She knew he had gone to the party as well. What if he didn't know? She did not want him to find out and rush off from his job in an emotional state of mind. She couldn't handle another accident. As it turned out, Bobby had decided not to go to work that day so he was at home when his friend called him with the news. Since Bobby lived right down the road from where the accident occurred, the responsibility of identifying the body had fallen on him.

Upon arrival at the fire station, their fears were confirmed and they immediately wanted to see Billy. After being informed that it would take some time for the funeral home to prepare his body, the family returned home to Guy and Jo-Anne's house. The news had already spread in their close-knit community and there were many friends and family there to lend their support. When they walked in the door, the first thing they did was embrace their younger son, Bobby. He, too, was having a difficult time dealing with the situation because he and Billy had a close relationship.

Although it seemed like a lifetime, in reality it had been three tormenting hours before the funeral home called to notify Guy and Jo-Anne they could come and see their son. Finally, they stood before Billy and the tears flowed freely. Being a mother, Jo-Anne couldn't bear to leave her son's side. She stood over him, rubbing his head and kissing his cheek. Guy found it impossible to handle as he rocked back and forth. His brother, Pete, gently walked

♥ He Blew Her a Kiss

him out of the room and sat him down. Pete's wife Donna had to assist with the rest of the arrangements.

The eight months following the funeral, Guy was in pure survival mode. Coping with the loss was taking a terrible toll on him. He became desperate to make contact with his son somehow. There was no question in his mind. It was something he had to do. He didn't know how, but he knew how much he needed that connection. At his wife's suggestion, they went to visit a spirit messenger named Vicki Monroe. It was Feb. 16, 2005, and that one visit changed their lives forever. Through Vicki they were able to make the connection with Billy that would spark an ongoing series of communications. Billy reassured them he was happy, safe, and healthy. The most important message he wanted to share was not to continue grieving for him. He urged them to move ahead with their lives. Billy shared the details of his accident on the ATV and how everything happened. Although his death was a loss to many, he explained his job here on earth had been completed and it had been his time to go home, to Heaven. This meaningful experience not only reassured them, but it uplifted them, especially Guy.

Two months after their comforting encounter, Guy found himself surfing the Internet. He avidly read everything he could about signs our loved ones can give us after they pass on. One thing that seemed to stand out

Love Shines Bright ♥

to him was how they can communicate through photos. So, Guy embarked on a new passion. He began taking random photographs just to see what might happen. In the very first photos, he discovered the truth to what he had read. His random pictures revealed what he believed to be spirit light dotting the image. That was at the end of April 2005.

It only took a few months for Guy to realize this would be a special journey. His purpose was to share this news with others and to encourage the belief that our loved one's spirits were still with us. We are not alone in this life we live. Through his endeavors, he has captured many various types of spirit images such as orbs, spirit essence, moving light, and angel light. Some of his most cherished images, though, are his pictures of the moon, street lights, and Christmas tree lights that appear heart-shaped. He considers these to be a special sign from his beloved son, Billy. Out of the thousands of pictures Guy has taken during the past three years, his ultimate favorite is a photo of the moon taken on Oct. 21, 2005. The moon appears in the perfect shape of a heart. You can see many of these photos on their website, www.oursonbilly.com.

The incredible journey Guy has embarked on and his amazing photos have had a profound effect upon his life. The inspiring images have given him focus and a purpose. After the initial shock, then the devastating reality

♥ He Blew Her a Kiss

of Billy's death, Guy fell into a deep depression. He was distraught and became quite withdrawn, wanting to sleep as much as possible. Being able to communicate with his son through a spirit mediator was the only thing that penetrated the cloud of despair that clung to him, smothering his ability to cope. That communication with Billy sparked a new path and an entirely new way of thinking. Although none of his actions could bring Billy back, Guy's collection of photos has brought him great comfort and a reassuring belief in the afterlife. The simple message they convey is love. The simple message Billy conveys is love. Realizing our loved ones are close by can be a comfort to all. They want us to be happy, continue moving forward, and most importantly, live our lives to the fullest.

~ Submitted by Guy Dusseault
www.facebook.com/groups/SignsFromOurLovedOnes
www.oursonbilly.com

Butterfly Kisses

Thinking back on her childhood, the thought of "butterfly kisses" always enchanted Denise. When she was a little girl, her mother demonstrated how they would feel by gently brushing her eyelashes across her cheek. It never failed to tickle Denise and leave her giggling. Of course when she became a mother, she shared it with her young daughter Jennifer with exactly the same results. Jennifer would giggle, laugh, and beg her mother to do it again.

As the years flew by, Jennifer grew to be a beautiful young lady. She had a special gift, among many. She was a brilliant conversationalist, able to hold someone under her spell for hours, even someone she just met. Jennifer also loved her family unconditionally. She totally adored

♥ He Blew Her a Kiss

her younger sibling Shayna, and together they shared a special bond only sisters can have.

Eventually children grow up, and the scariest time for parents is when a child leaves the nest. Venturing out into the world, their safety becomes a prevalent concern. Denise had faced those emotions when her oldest daughter moved away from home to attend Brooklyn College. Even though concerned for her daughter's well-being, she was extremely proud of the young adult Jennifer was becoming.

One day, Denise received the phone call that would forever change their lives. Jennifer, her beautiful daughter, had suffered an asthma attack. She was alone in her apartment, so by the time the paramedics were able to gain entry it was too late. Jennifer was gone.

At the cemetery, Denise quietly excused herself to go to the restroom. Walking alone she noticed a beautiful small yellow butterfly. To her amazement, it kept flying by brushing against her cheek. Nothing like that had ever happened to her. When she came back out, to her surprise, the butterfly was still there patiently waiting. God's tiny little creature escorted her back to her husband Steve and their daughter Shayna. Denise had finally been blessed by "butterfly kisses," and in her heart she knew it was a gift from God, allowing Jennifer to kiss her good-bye.

The following month, Denise and her family left for

their annual beach vacation to Ogunquit, Maine. Jennifer had always accompanied them to this beautiful place by the sea she loved so much. Denise knew it would be difficult, but she felt Jennifer would be there with them and she was right. As they were closing the car doors in the beach parking lot, that same beautiful small yellow butterfly swooshed down and brushed its fragile wings against Shayna's cheek. She too received a good-bye kiss from her big sister.

Now Denise and her family keep a watchful eye out for their beautiful yellow butterfly. It has become a symbol to them that Jennifer is safe and happy. Denise is also very thankful God provided them a much needed moment of comfort through something as delicate and unique as "butterfly kisses."

~ Submitted by Denise Sommer

A Christmas Spirit of Love

One cold winter evening in 1998, Pam was snug and secure in her living room engaged in a labor of love. Her husband happened to be out of town, but she didn't mind. She welcomed the occasional solitude because those times allowed her to indulge in activities that relaxed her. This particular evening, her project was a baby dress she was smocking for her granddaughter.

As the television droned in the background, her hands performed their task skillfully, almost without thought. Sitting in her favorite chair, she felt a sudden brush of air across her face and instantly the scent of her paternal grandmother filled the room. She stopped and playfully exclaimed, "Grandma, is that you? I bet you came to see what I'm making!" Hunny, Pam's nickname given by her

♥ He Blew Her a Kiss

family, knew her grandma was right there with her watching with pride. Grandma, being a seamstress, had played a huge role in teaching Hunny to sew at an early age. Her presence and scent was a familiar and overwhelming comfort. As Hunny continued smocking, her mind reminisced on many evenings spent with her grandma.

Later, Hunny retired to bed at her usual time. Nestling her head into the pillow, she replayed the amazing encounter with her grandma. It had been such a wonderful comfort just having her near again. Before Hunny could even finish her thoughts, it happened again. She felt her grandma's presence close to her pillow and again that familiar scent. Hunny instinctively knew Grandma was kneeling at the head of the bed saying a prayer on behalf of her granddaughter.

As a young girl, Hunny had overheard Grandma praying for her children and grandchildren for what seemed like hours each night. Even the arthritis that wreaked havoc on her knees couldn't prevent her from kneeling in reverence and lifting her loved ones to God in prayer. Grandma was a true prayer warrior, and Hunny knew in her heart she was still interceding on her behalf. This day would be one to cherish for a lifetime.

Grandma obviously still loved Christmas time because only a few days later she came to visit again. This time Hunny was busy in the kitchen baking Christmas goodies, and could smell Grandma over the scent of cookies and candies baking. She missed her so much, and felt like Grandma wanted to be a part of this special day. Conversation seemed only natural. It did occur to Hunny that if anyone walked in while she was having these conversations, they would surely think she had lost her mind. She chuckled to herself thinking how it must look, but she didn't really care. She would be forever grateful for the comfort and blessing she received from those visits. Sometimes she thinks Grandma has never left. Maybe she hasn't!

~ Submitted by Pam Boswell

A Song of Love

Steeped in traditions, the Greek people place great emphasis on four key elements to their life: a deep commitment to family, a steadfast faith in their religion, a robust love of food, and last, but not least, their passion for music. Each element plays an integral part in their everyday life. Steven had the privilege of growing up with such a rich heritage that had been handed down generation to generation.

Aside from the support and encouragement his parents had always provided, Steven was blessed to have his grandmother near. He lovingly referred to her as Yia-Yia (Yah-Yah), which is the Greek word for grandmother. Many a night he would sit and play the guitar for her. She would quietly listen, tapping her foot to the melodic

♥ He Blew Her a Kiss

sounds as his hand strummed across the strings. As each song came to an end, with love shining in her eyes, she would proudly exclaim, "Bravo, Stavros." Yia-Yia always called him by his Greek name. Steven cherished the time he was able to spend with her.

When Yia-Yia passed away, Steven's heart was saddened. He would miss her terribly, but at the same time he was relieved to know that she would no longer be suffering. On the same evening that she passed, he sat in the living room pondering her life and reflecting on all the love she had shown him and how important those memories were.

Suddenly Steven heard a soft yet very distinctive voice he recognized immediately. It was Yia-Yia and, to his amazement, she was singing a song to him. In all the times he had played the guitar and sung for her, she had never joined in, so he listened intently to every word.

> "In death you will not find me for I'm in my Father's house.
> Please look past my body and see his light throughout.
> I'm here with you in spirit, accept my gift of love.
> Rejoice I am in heaven with our Father above.
> Life is a journey filled with earthly tasks.
> Remember, when you need me you only have to ask.
> I'm here with you in spirit and with our Father, too,
> joyously in heaven eternally with you!"

A Song of Love ♥

Steven quickly ran over and immediately flipped on his tape recorder and sang the song just as Yia-Yia had sung it to him. He then gave his mother a copy of the tape. In keeping with Greek tradition, there is a visitation time, or gathering, prior to the funeral. They then have a dinner after the burial. His mother was so touched by the song she played it for everyone in attendance. You could hear a pin drop as each person focused upon the words and everyone agreed it was a meaningful and beautiful message. Their shared belief on what happens to our soul after this earthly departure was reinforced through the heartfelt message from a soul that was filled with peace and joy.

Steven had the presence of mind to have those words copy-written, and to this day shares his heavenly message with others during their time of loss so they, too, will find comfort in what is to come. He respectfully thanks his Yia-Yia for sharing her song of love.

~ Submitted by Steven Lourakis

The Irises Are Blooming

Fulfilling her annual tradition, Elaine strolled through her mother's yard admiring the bright fresh blooms eagerly drinking up the sun's rays. An incredible aroma filled the air as the scent from a multitude of flowers floated on the breeze. Her mother's garden was always a wonderful place to be. The rainbow of colors gave the yard a happy, cheerful appearance that seemed to transfer the same feelings to whoever was near. Her mother was proud of the garden that had taken years for her to cultivate and loved showing it off. She was particularly fond of her irises.

Elaine, in an effort to duplicate her mother's success, had planted many iris bulbs in her own yard but sadly never achieved the results she envisioned. Her plants

♥ He Blew Her a Kiss

would come up year after year but, because of an abundance of shade, she was never able to enjoy the beauty of her own blooms. In spite of the disappointment of her own garden, Elaine was thankful for the opportunity to spend time with her mother in hers. Within the sanctuary of her mother's flowers, all past differences between the two seemed to disappear.

Like all mothers and daughters, Elaine and her mother had their share of disparities. At a younger age, she had felt some justification for placing blame on her mother for her parents' divorce. It was more than 20 years ago and even though it had been a problem for Elaine, she had long since gotten over it. As time progressed, their relationship blossomed into one of mutual respect and a deep love for one another. Elaine recognized how much of a blessing it was to have her mother to call upon, not only for advice but for everyday conversation as well.

One hot June evening around 8 p.m., Elaine unknowingly had her last conversation with her mother. They discussed nothing out of the ordinary. It was just a typical conversation like many before. When the phone rang at 10 that same evening, Elaine didn't think twice when she answered and it was her stepfather. She assumed when he told her she needed to come over because "she" was sick, he was referring to Elaine's granddaughter who was staying the night with them. Elaine was in no hurry as she changed from her pajamas into her clothes and combed her hair. She told her husband they had to pick up their granddaughter so she could be taken to the doctor the following morning.

As they got closer to her mother's house, an ambulance passed them headed in the direction they had just come. It didn't appear to be an emergency because the sirens were silent, the lights weren't flashing, and they didn't seem to be in a rush. Elaine was quite surprised when they pulled up to the house to see her stepfather and his family standing in the front yard. She pondered what could be going on. As soon as she exited the car, they informed her that her mother was gone. It was hard for her mind to grasp that concept since they had just spoken a few hours ago. When the reality did set in, Elaine realized the words they had shared earlier were the last ones she would ever share with her mother. Even though she couldn't have foreseen what was going to happen, she still regretted the missed opportunity to tell her mother, among other things, how much she loved her.

The morning of the funeral came and the weather reflected the sadness everyone felt in their hearts. It was dark, gray, and overcast. As the procession made its way to the cemetery, the rain began to fall from the heavens like a multitude of tears. Elaine's heart sank even further but she prayed silently, "Oh dear Lord, please hold off

♥ He Blew Her a Kiss

the rain so that all these people will be able to stay for the funeral." Just like that, the rain stopped. Everyone paid their last respects, and as soon as the graveside service was finished and people were in their cars, the rain began to fall again. Elaine knew God had heard her prayer and she had just witnessed what her heart knew was a miracle.

Each day after the funeral was challenging. Many friends tried to give her words of comfort, and she knew they all meant well but it was still painful. Instinctively, Elaine found herself reaching for the phone to call her mother every time something came up. The stark reality that she could no longer pick up the phone and talk to her mother left her a bit out of sorts. It was the little things that made the days so difficult. She missed her mother terribly.

Within the same year her mother died, Elaine's stepfather sold the house. This upset her a little. What would become of her mother's beautiful gardens? Sadly, it was only a matter of months before her stepfather passed as well. Elaine knew her mother was not particularly a religious person so she worried about where exactly her mother was. Every day she would pray to God asking for a sign her mother was with Him and she was all right. Time slowly passed but she never gave up on receiving a sign.

The Irises Are Blooming ♥

The first spring after her mother's death, Elaine decided to drive to her mother's old house to see if her flower beds were being tended. To her complete dismay, all the flowers were gone. There wasn't a single plant left. The house looked disheveled and forgotten. Elaine just couldn't comprehend why anyone would do this. Surely this could not possibly be the sign for which she had so diligently asked. With complete dejection, she headed back to her own home.

That same spring, although subtle at first, Elaine began noticing small changes in her own yard. Each day she would see more and more of her irises blooming. She was amazed because these exact flowers had never ever bloomed before and she had done absolutely nothing different. It wasn't long until her yard was just as beautiful as her mother's had always been. Her friends and neighbors were astonished at the transformation and pleaded with her to share with them what she had done to resurrect them. Even the flowers in the shade proudly displayed their ornate beauty.

Elaine didn't share any secret gardening tips because she had none to give. The profusion of blooms emerging from what had always been barren plants had to be the sign for which she had fervently prayed. At last, she could rest assured her mother was right there in Heaven safe and secure in the love of her creator. Further testament

♥ He Blew Her a Kiss

that this was her sign was the fact that since that spring her flowers have never bloomed again. God works in mysterious and creative ways.

As Elaine marveled at the unique sign God had chosen to give her, she never again questioned where or how her mother was. She knew in her heart that her mother was happily cultivating a garden of unimaginable beauty in a better place. Elaine was equally sure that out of all the beautiful flowers her mother was surely tending to, the iris was still her favorite. The sign had indeed helped her release the hurt she had been struggling with and made her realize how happy her mother must be now.

~ Submitted by Elaine Blakley

A Father's Love Is Forever

Sal D'Incecco was a vibrant and passionate man. The Italian blood coursing through his veins made him the typical protective and strict, but very loving family man. Sometimes difficult to please, everyone who knew him understood, without it having to be said, they could count on him no matter what. His actions did the talking for him. A bit on the eccentric side, Sal was unique and sometimes intense. People either loved him or they didn't. There was no in between. There was a special place in Sal's heart for his daughters so, needless to say, they shared a special bond. For Suzanne, he was her knight in shining armor and there was nothing he wouldn't do for either of them.

Sal was a jack of all trades, knowledgeable in almost every field. A modern-day Michelangelo, he spent 10

♥ He Blew Her a Kiss

years building a miniature carousel in his garage. It was one-seventh the scale of a full-sized carousel; nine feet in diameter, six feet high, and weighing in at one ton. The carousel had been a particular passion of his and he took great care to be meticulous with the details. Each piece, including the 60 horses, was hand-carved. It was breathtaking to see it complete in its full glory, particularly after seeing him invest so many years and so much of himself into it. His patience and determination resulted in a beautiful masterpiece in miniature. It was only fitting that something so beautiful should be seen by others.

The mayor of Mount Kisco, New York, shared that belief and was happy to unveil it to the public. The culmination of Sal's dedication and commitment to perfection was proudly displayed at the local mall. It touched his heart that families from all over the area were able to appreciate its beauty. Although Suzanne and her father were at odds at the time all this came about, she loved her father and had never been so proud of him. In spite of their disagreement she always considered her father amazing, and this only served to strengthen that belief.

Sal was a compassionate man as well, especially when it came to animals. On one occasion, he nurtured an injured deer he found on the road back to health. Many times he saved and cared for baby birds that had fallen

A Father's Love Is Forever ♥

from their nests. He had a deep affinity for all birds and had several exotic birds of his own. His favorite by far was Lola, a Gotham cockatoo. She was testy and unforgiving to others but she loved Sal. They seemed to have a special understanding of one another. Lola happily spent much of her time perched on his shoulder. He would play games with his birds like peek-a-boo, and then cradle them in his arms gently caressing their bellies. His birds brought him great pleasure and happiness.

Suzanne was proud of her father in every way. He was always such a strong influence in her life, and together they shared an unbreakable bond. He served not only as a father, but a mentor, an advisor, and most of all her hero. When Sal received the news he had blood cancer, the emotional stability of not only Suzanne, but the entire family as well, was shattered. What would happen to their family? She knew nothing would ever be the same. Devoted to her father, she was constantly at his side. Her vigilance never swayed. Suzanne was grateful her husband Frank was so supportive during this time because it allowed her to spend every precious moment possible with the father she loved so much. His decline accelerated much too quickly, and a short two months later he passed away. None of this seemed fair no matter how hard she tried to make sense of it. Even with all the support of her family, her heart ached with the pain of his loss.

♥ He Blew Her a Kiss

    It wasn't long after his death that Sal began communicating with Suzanne through signs. She had never really heard or read about after-death communication, so at first she actually thought she was hallucinating. She thought maybe it was brought on by the stress and grief she was experiencing after his death. The strange thing about it, though, was each time it occurred she felt relief and comfort. At first, her father would appear to her in what seemed like dreams. They were so vivid and locked into her memory, though, unlike her usual scattered dreams. He repeatedly gave her the same message he was not dead. Even though it felt peaceful, she knew the reality was he couldn't possibly be alive because she was there when he passed away. None of it was making any sense to her. Her mother and sister were quick to dismiss it and claimed she was just in denial of his loss. But this truly felt different. She sought out other counsel from mediums she had checked out and they confirmed her father was near her. It was comforting holding on to that thought, whether she believed it was true or not.

    One particular instance, Suzanne had fallen asleep when she actually felt his embrace. Her father hugged her and told her he was all right. In her heart, she just knew it wasn't a dream. It was a real, tangible feeling. When she awoke she felt refreshingly at peace and truly felt his presence. She began feeling a little bit better each time something happened. Months later, Sal appeared again and she vividly remembered him looking so young and healthy. She had a distinct feeling of leaving her body and being transported to another place. She couldn't describe it other than the intense peace and feeling of love she experienced. Then just as quickly, it was over. She remembered thinking, maybe this is what heaven feels like. All the pain and grief that had become a part of her had just melted away. The last time he physically appeared to her was when she fell asleep on her couch. Suddenly, he was right next to her sharing that he had to go now. She sensed his visits might stop, but knowing her father like she did, her heart was convinced his spirit would never be far from her.

Indeed the visits stopped, but Sal still had other signs in store for her. It was Suzanne's birthday and she was particularly preoccupied with the absence of him. She had driven up into the Catskills to eat at a restaurant she loved. While waiting outside for a table, her thoughts went to her daddy and she wished so much he could be there with her to celebrate. As reality set in, tears crept into her eyes. She then looked up to find the waitress had arrived notifying that her table was ready. As Suzanne followed her into the restaurant, she noticed the music softly playing over the speakers. It was the song "Daddy's Home." She felt an involuntary smile forming and thought to herself, my daddy played that for me.

♥ He Blew Her a Kiss

Suzanne, now even more curious about all the incidences that were occurring with her father, began investigating more and eventually came across a website dedicated to such experiences. She received detailed explanations as to what the signs were and found, contrary to what others thought about her, she was not going crazy and she was not hallucinating. These signs come to literally millions of people. Some people are open to them and yet others overlook them because they lack the belief that such communication can happen. Some signs are dramatic while some can be a bit more subtle. Relieved to discover this newfound knowledge, Suzanne was confident her father was near. Finished with her investigating one night, she headed downstairs to the kitchen, where a most profound sign occurred and was witnessed by her entire family.

Suzanne had visited a psychic medium on what would have been Sal's 64th birthday. The medium said her father had birds around him and suggested she purchase a wind chime with birds on it. She also gave her specific instructions to hang them in a place where no possible disturbances could occur. So, shortly after, Suzanne took her advice and purchased chimes adorned with birds and hung it in the kitchen. Nothing out of the ordinary happened right away. In fact, many months passed and the chimes had become just another fixture in the room. One

A Father's Love Is Forever ♥

morning, however, when Suzanne entered the kitchen, her glance fell on the chimes and they were completely tangled up. She stopped in her tracks, amazed at what she saw. There was no wind in her kitchen, nothing that would disrupt the chimes. She asked everyone in the family and no one had touched them. She knew immediately this was confirmation from her father that what she had just learned about signs was true.

For the majority of the day, the chimes remained tangled. Finally that evening, almost in a joking kind of way, she called out to her father, "Daddy, you better fix the chimes." An hour later they were untangled, hanging as they had always been, looking completely undisturbed. Once again the family had not touched them. Her son and daughter, stirred up by all the excitement, called out, "Grandpa, do it again!" Already amazed it had happened twice Suzanne did not expect anything more and returned upstairs. Several minutes later her son called out, "Mommy, Mommy, the chimes!" Frank, Arianna, and Suzanne hurried downstairs and sure enough they were changed again, only this time crisscrossed in the form of Xs.

Frank, her husband who was a self-proclaimed skeptic, was amazed and speechless about what had just occurred in their home. He could find no other logical explanation for the chimes changing as they had. Suzanne

♥ He Blew Her a Kiss

was so thrilled this sign had been witnessed by the entire family. It served to validate everything she had learned about after-death communication. For them, it was undeniable proof her father's presence was real. Today these chimes remain in the home just as he left them. They are a constant reminder to Suzanne and the rest of the family that her father, and his love, is always with them each and every day.

On numerous occasions, Suzanne felt the presence of her father. She experienced several different kinds of signs, and even though she was confused at first, she quickly came to accept and appreciate them for what they were. She drew comfort from the feelings they evoked even though these signs could not logically be explained. Suzanne's deep love and trust in her father were merely reinforced by his communications. In life, he had always been her champion, steadfast and true. And even after his death, he continued to show his precious little girl a father's love is forever.

~ Submitted by Suzanne DiBuono

The Healing House

Debbie was an only child but she never felt alone. Both of her parents loved her very much so, growing up, they referred to themselves as the "Three Musketeers." They did everything together. They played, laughed, and cried when necessary. Through thick and thin, they knew they could count on one another for anything. The close relationship they shared resulted in a multitude of happy memories that Debbie would carry throughout her life.

Debbie had always been a daddy's girl, but after her mother died in 1988 their bond strengthened tenfold. They were no longer the "Three Musketeers." It was now just the two of them and they grew even closer. Not only was he her father, he was also her friend. They relied on

♥ He Blew Her a Kiss

each other so much but were happy to be there for one another. To a daughter, fathers represent strength, someone they can always count on. Dad is the one you turn to when anything needs fixing. And her father had never let her down. After years of being her hero, the time had finally come when he had to depend upon her. His body had grown weaker as his age progressed and even simple tasks required assistance. Trips to the doctor proved to be somewhat futile since there was no cure for growing old. However, there were times when hospital stays were necessary.

As Debbie transported her father home from his most recent stay at the hospital, anxiety began to build up inside her. There was an almost tangible sense of foreboding that the time he had left would be very limited, so she decided to stay overnight. As Debbie helped her father get comfortable, she realized how thankful she was to still have him with her. She cherished the opportunity to give back to her father what he had bestowed upon her for so many years. His love, compassion, and deep loyalty were the foundation of their relationship, and Debbie considered herself blessed. She also was thankful for being back in her childhood home that had nurtured such warm, loving memories within its comforting walls.

As evening fell upon them, Debbie decided to make a pallet on the floor next to her father's bed. She wanted to be close at hand in case he woke during the night and needed her. With her two dogs lying at her feet and the lights dimmed down, she finally drifted to sleep. At approximately 2:30 in the morning Debbie felt her dog Willow get up. She watched as Willow walked around the bed, then came back and settled down. Since she was awake, Debbie decided to check on her dad. As she approached his bed, she realized he was dying. It was as if Willow had sensed it. Debbie would be forever thankful for that because it allowed her to be right there holding her father as he took his last breath. She wanted him to know that he was not alone.

After her father passed on Dec. 5, 2007, Debbie was faced with the dilemma of what to do with their family home. It had always provided her with happy memories, but now she was afraid it would feel empty with her father gone. At the same time, she did not want to sell the home. She really didn't know what she was going to do. Shortly after her father died she got a phone call from a friend going through an unwanted divorce. She needed a place to stay and Debbie was happy to help her out. It actually worked out quite well for the both of them.

For Debbie's friend, having a place to stay was an answered prayer. The divorce had turned her life upside down and she needed time to heal and get her life back together. It turned out her new residence was the perfect

♥ He Blew Her a Kiss

place for her to be. The home seemed to radiate the love and comfort its former residents had always demonstrated. It was as if their presence surrounded her. She found herself becoming stronger and more independent. After only a year, she was able to move out and buy her own home. She expressed her thanks to Debbie and credited the family home for her speedy recovery.

At the same time her friend was moving out, Debbie was battling various problems in her own home. Discovering mold from a troublesome leak in her roof proved to be the last straw. Repairs would take some time and the contractor highly recommended she vacate the premises for the duration of the work. It turned out to be perfect timing for Debbie. Although thankful for having her parents' home to go to, she was still apprehensive about being there alone.

At first, it felt a little strange and she was thankful for the companionship of her two dogs. But, after more time she spent settling in, the home seemed to welcome her even more. Debbie found that although her father was physically gone, she could still feel the overwhelming comfort of his presence. Oftentimes during her stay, she would suddenly have her father's scent envelope her. Those were the times she was transported back to when they were together and happy. Her stay there confirmed her childhood belief that Daddy could fix anything.

The Healing House ♥

At the time Debbie was not only coping with the loss of her father, she was also trying to recover from a four-year relationship that had recently ended. In his own special way, Debbie knew her father was still watching over her and his love filled her with the strength and confidence she needed to move forward. Being there in the healing house surrounded by the love of her father proved to be the best decision she'd ever made. Now she can live her life secure in the knowledge that love knows no boundaries. Our loved ones, though no longer present in body, continue to love and watch over us as we fulfill our life's purpose. Debbie is comforted by the belief that when the time comes, the "Three Musketeers" will once again be reunited.

~ Submitted by Debbie Overton

The Journey Begins

Suzanne was proud of her accomplished career in the navy, but after witnessing firsthand the destruction during the terrorist attack on 9/11, the importance of life really hit home. Experiencing a shift in her priorities, she learned, as so many others did, not to take life for granted. It was then she made the choice to retire along with her husband, Ty, who also had enjoyed a distinguished career in the navy. Military service was in fact a family affair. Suzanne's stepdaughter, Susan, had chosen a career in the marines, where she met and married her husband, Warren. Service and commitment infused the very fiber of their beings, yet they never lost sight of the importance of loved ones. Family meant everything.

Suzanne and Ty were thrilled to be sailing the oceans

♥ He Blew Her a Kiss

of the world on their own time. Their home away from home was a 46-foot sailboat dubbed "Liberty." How appropriate considering the freedom they now felt to indulge the passion they both shared. It was during a relaxed trip, destination Venice, when a tragedy occurred that would prove to be the catalyst for a life-changing transformation. Suzanne and Ty were devastated when their son-in-law Warren informed them of the inconceivable events that led to Susan's untimely death. Following is an excerpt from her book *Messages of Hope*.

> On a sunny June day my stepdaughter Susan was taken from us by a bolt of lightning that came out of the blue. My husband Ty and I had been sailing in the Mediterranean when we received the devastating news. Returning to our sailboat in Croatia and adjusting to life without Susan the week after her funeral was difficult. I filled the empty moments by reading several books about life after death that I'd bought on the way to the airport.
>
> The next morning we got under way and headed south, anxious to leave Croatia and our bad memories behind. By then, I had finished one book and began the second book to which I'd been led. I'd read books by mediums in the past, but always out of mere curiosity. Now I read with growing excitement the

The Journey Begins ♥

seemingly irrefutable evidence that life doesn't end with the death of the physical body.

Two days into our southerly passage, I'd finished most of book number two. I sat in the cockpit reading the final pages as Ty manned the helm.

"Hey, Suzanne," *he said.*

I looked up.

"Have you noticed the yellow butterfly that's been following us for the past two days?"

I looked aft and spotted it. In fact, I had noticed it, but lost in my thoughts, I hadn't paid attention. Now I realized how unusual it was to see a butterfly so far out on the water. I glanced at the shoreline, a thin blue line in the distance. The nearest land was a good four miles away.

"I wonder what it's doing way out here," *I said.*

"Kind of strange," *Ty said.*

I went back to my book, and there, on the very page I'd been reading when Ty interrupted me, was a message straight from heaven.

"My God," *I said for the second time in a week,* "listen to this..."

I read aloud the author George Anderson's timely claim that "signs from the Infinite Light can often be right under our noses . . . as subtle as a tiny butterfly in December."

Ty blinked in surprise, looked aft, and said, "Or on the Adriatic Sea?"

I went on to read aloud Anderson's story of a woman who began seeing ubiquitous yellow butterflies shortly after the death of her son. At that moment, the butterfly that had fluttered back and forth in our wake for two days drew even with the cockpit where we sat then flew directly between Ty and me before heading for shore.

Was it a coincidence? A fluke of nature? If so, then so was the swarm of yellow butterflies that hovered overhead as we arrived at the island of Mljet later that day. Six other boats lined the sea wall beside us, yet ours was the only one with the yellow winged visitors who made their presence known for half an hour on that very special evening.

The next day, rather than get under way right away, Ty and I set out on a hike. A winding path led through thick woods to the island's highest point. Still dazed and numb from Susan's death, we walked in silence. Instead of staring at my feet, I stared pointedly at the trail ahead. By then I'd read dozens of accounts in books describing wispy figures that appeared to those who were grieving. As we trudged upward, I willed Susan to make her presence known to me.

Higher and higher we climbed, and with each step

I grew more despondent. Why couldn't I sense her? Surely all the miraculous stories I'd read pointed to some kind of existence after death. We reached the summit and turned to retrace our steps. Ty walked on ahead of me now, a good fifty yards down the trail. Discouraged, but not defeated, I continued my efforts. "Susan," I prayed, "please give me some kind of sign that you're around. We so desperately need to know that you're not gone forever."

Knowing what I know now about the spirit world, I can just picture Susan at that moment. I'm sure she was shaking her head at me, laughing, and saying, "Haven't you noticed all the butterflies I've been sending you?"

Susan was laughing because just then, a flicker of movement from the left caught my attention. I turned my head and saw a yellow butterfly with a red dot on its back flying straight at me. It arrived at my side, flew a complete circle around me, and then bounced straight into my chest at the level of my heart. I stopped in my tracks and watched, stunned, as the butterfly then flew in a direct line down the trail toward Ty. Incredulous, I called out his name. The shock in my voice caused him to stop and turn. The butterfly had reached him by then, and I watched as it flew a complete circle around him, as well, before bouncing into what would

♥ He Blew Her a Kiss

have been his chest had I not caused him to turn so suddenly. As it was, the butterfly touched him right at the level of his heart, before flying off into the woods.

I stood rooted in place, awestruck, and reviewed the unusual events of the past two days: the butterfly that accompanied us for two days at sea, the special swarm around our boat, and now a butterfly that flew a specific and meaningful path, as if being guided. I may be a bit slow at times, but I finally got it. I wasn't able to sense Susan's spirit directly, but somehow—perhaps with the assistance of more experienced helpers on the other side—she'd been sending us signs in direct answer to my prayers. I continued down the trail, my steps a bit lighter. There was no doubt in my mind that something spiritual was going on and that Susan was behind it.*

For Suzanne, her transformation began after refusing to believe someone as vibrant, passionate, and loving as her stepdaughter Susan could just simply cease to exist. What really happens to the spirit, the soul of an individual? Searching for answers, Suzanne sought out a medium who uncannily described Susan, whom she had never met nor did she know anything about. With a background similar to a scientist, Suzanne had always looked at things in black and white. Shades of gray had never before existed in her mind. This changed everything. After experiencing her own after-death communications with the stepdaughter she loved so much, Suzanne felt the peace and comfort in the knowledge that our spirits live on, one day to be reunited. One step at a time, Suzanne began a journey that has forever changed her life.

* Excerpted from the book *Messages of Hope* by Suzanne Giesemann, available from www.OneMindBooks.com or wherever books are sold.

~ Submitted by Suzanne Giesemann

Hello, I'm Still Here

Having a child oftentimes changes your entire perception about life. Suddenly, you are responsible for the care, protection, and nurturing of a helpless little soul. The foundation you help establish in your child's life is what they will build their future upon. As a parent, you naturally want what's best for them. Glenda felt this way and when her son Chad was only six months old, she gave her life over to God. She promised to raise him the best she could and instruct him according to God's word. As her little boy grew, she was true to her word and spent a great deal of time with him. They played games that were not only fun, but would also help prepare him for life. Over the years and watchful eyes of his parents, Chad grew into quite the gentleman. Being self-confident

♥ He Blew Her a Kiss

and genuine, he made friends quite easily and touched many lives. His entire persona was one of sincerity and compassion with a healthy respect for life and nature. Armed with impeccable values and a close relationship to God, there was no doubt their son was destined to have a happy and fulfilled life.

Chad was fortunate enough to have the opportunity to study overseas in London. Although Glenda and Larry were very proud and excited for him, they still felt a little apprehensive about him being so far from home, much less out of the country. Nevertheless, they saw him off with love, praise, and lots of hugs. Just as any parent would do, they reminded him to be careful out there on his own. And, so off to London he went. Phone calls home were filled with excitement as he recounted his adventures overseas. He was so happy and upbeat, his enthusiasm was contagious. The loving bond Glenda and her husband shared with Chad was evident as they rejoiced in his happiness. But all that was soon to change.

Larry was closest to the phone when it rang that fateful evening. The tone in her husband's voice caught Glenda's attention almost instantly. She was terrified as she watched Larry's knees buckle underneath him. The long-distance call brought news of their son Chad's death. Tragically, he had been struck by a car and did not survive his injuries. All Glenda knew was it felt as if all the

Hello, I'm Still Here ♥

air had been sucked from the room. Realizing this was not some bad dream she would wake from, Glenda felt her heart crumble into a million pieces. Once the shock began to slowly release her from its grasp, all she could think was, "Why God, why Chad? I'm not supposed to outlive my son." The harsh reality felt as if it had physically beaten her up. That one phone call changed their lives forever. That night, as Glenda lay balled up in the bed with tears streaming down her face, she tried desperately to get some rest. It seemed to be a futile attempt, when all of a sudden she saw Chad in a cloud looking at her. He looked so real. She heard his voice as he said, "Mom, please don't cry. I didn't want to leave you and Dad, but Grandpa and the others convinced me that I wouldn't be the same if I stayed, so I left with them. I am here and I am safe and I will always be with you." With the words replaying in her mind Glenda drifted off to sleep.

For 21 years, it had been the three of them. Larry and Glenda enjoyed a special bond with their son parents feel so blessed to have. Because of their closeness, Glenda realized her son was getting pretty serious in his relationship with his girlfriend, Jennifer. Although she wasn't in any hurry, Glenda had prepared herself somewhat to release her son with her blessings. But this, this was something completely different. How was she going to handle never seeing Chad again? It was a horrifying prospect she

♥ He Blew Her a Kiss

struggled with daily. In an effort to combat the sadness and feeling of emptiness, Larry and Glenda spent time doing things together. Somehow that made everything a little more bearable. They went grocery shopping and to the movies, but her favorite activity was taking long drives together. It provided the perfect opportunity to shed tears without anyone else noticing her.

One evening she and Larry had gone to a movie. Excusing herself to go to the restroom, she walked in and immediately surveyed her surroundings. It was relatively small, but looking at the counter and sink she felt as if it were fairly clean. After taking care of business, she exited the stall and walked over to the sink to wash her hands. There on the counter lay a diamond ring. No one else had entered the bathroom while she was there, and it certainly wasn't there when she came in. Picking it up she realized it was identical to the ring Chad had given his girlfriend before the tragic accident. Glenda immediately went to the management at the theater to see if anyone had reported losing a ring. They all replied "no," so she took it with her. She felt it only appropriate to give it to Chad's girlfriend. In her heart, she believed this was her son's way of telling Jennifer, "I love you."

It helped Larry and Glenda to maintain their relationship with Jennifer. In some small way, it made them feel closer to their son. Four and a half years after Chad had passed, they truly wanted the best for her and wanted to see her happy again. In fact, they had introduced her to another young man she seemed to be getting along with quite well. Glenda was thrilled when she stopped by one night just to talk about the possibilities of her getting married. As they were sitting there chatting, the most amazing thing happened. The first time Jen uttered the word "marry" the back massager chair pad, which no one was sitting in, turned on by itself. After a few seconds it turned off. Subsequently, every time she mentioned getting married it came on and about 20 seconds later it would shut off. It frightened her to death every time, but Glenda just smiled and told her to say hello to Chad. With a shocked expression she said, "Is he really here?" Glenda replied, "He sure is and he's using electricity to show us." The chair turned on and off a total of four times, but once Jen said hello to Chad it stopped. By that point, she was totally amazed. Glenda believed Chad was showing his approval of the possible marriage.

Another thing her son loved to do was mess with the dog. Glenda would indulge their dog in friendly games of fetch. Throwing the ball down the long hallway, he would run like crazy to get it and bring it back, anxiously anticipating another throw. Occasionally on his return trip, the dog, with the ball safely tucked in his mouth, would just stop and sit, staring at the hall closet. No matter what

♥ He Blew Her a Kiss

Glenda did she could not distract him from the door. He refused to come to her. Finally, she would acknowledge Chad's presence and tell him to leave the dog alone. Immediately, the dog would return ready to play again. She knew this was crazy and didn't share these encounters with many people because of fear of what they might think, but she was definitely not imagining things.

Sometimes, when others are present to witness a sign, it helps to validate the experience. One day Glenda's friend Kay came by to watch a training video. Chad picked that moment to show up again. The remote was sitting on the table in front of Kay when the TV suddenly turned off. Kay looked at Glenda and asked her why she'd turned it off. Glenda began to smile and reminded her that the remote was sitting on the table. Then the TV came back on. After a few minutes, it did the same thing over again. This time Glenda said, "Chad, quit, you're scaring Kay." Kay looked at her with a strange expression on her face, then continued to watch the video. Then as if on cue, the set went off again. Glenda casually told her friend to say hello to Chad. He was there and just showing off for Kay. After she quickly said hello to him, the TV came back on and didn't go off the rest of the day.

Glenda has had many different experiences like the ones mentioned above. Growing up, her religious beliefs had never allowed for these types of encounters, but she never felt afraid of them. In her heart, she knew it was her precious son Chad just reminding her that he was near. It was comforting to know she had not lost him completely. Many times, on special occasions like her birthday or Chad's birthday, she would receive phone calls seemingly out of the blue. People that knew her son felt compelled to call and share a personal story of how he had touched their lives. They had no idea how much it truly meant for her to hear such heartwarming stories about Chad. They served as a gentle reminder of how wonderful his time on earth had been and how he had made the most out of every moment. She now pursues ways to help other parents cope with the pain and grief of losing a child. As Glenda sees it, we are eternal beings created to be eternal and our spirit self is never lost. When it's time we will see them again. Until then, if we remain open and willing we can receive messages. Love is the only thing we take with us when we pass and it continues through eternity.

~ Submitted by Glenda Pearson
Certified Grief Recovery Specialist
Author of *But Should the Angels Call for Him*
www.LivingThroughLoss.com

Fairy-Tale Love

Margaret's story could quite as easily start with "once upon a time..." Hers is a story that could rival any fairy-tale romance. When she and her husband Will met, they instinctively knew their soul had met its mate. Both had experienced previous marriages but this one would prove to be a forever love. As in any fairy tale, Margaret and Will spent every available moment together. Like two peas in a pod, they shared many common interests and loved spending time together. Their castle, a quaint home in the country, served to provide a peaceful retreat from the chaos of the outside world. For 19 years, they lived a life full of love, respect, and devotion.

One morning, like any normal workday, Will kissed his wife good-bye and headed out the door. Margaret always

♥ He Blew Her a Kiss

felt a tinge of worry each time he went to work. She was fully aware of the danger dealing with high-voltage transformers inherently held. For that reason, she was grateful each evening that he returned safely home.

This time Margaret's fears were realized. While servicing a transformer at Whiteface Mountain on the Lake Placid Olympic Grounds, Will had the extreme misfortune of being on the receiving end of an electrical arc. Although the occurrence of an arc is relatively infrequent, it typically proves to be fatal because the resulting fire from the current is reported to be four times hotter than the surface of the sun.

It was a dark and despondent time for Margaret. Will, her true Prince Charming, had always surrounded her with an impregnable circle of love. Together she knew they could conquer anything but now, after his death, she felt vulnerable. Each day was difficult to navigate without his presence. The tears and loneliness became her constant companions. At night she battled the overwhelming emptiness of which his side of the bed reminded her. She knew her life would continue, but would the pain ever subside?

About 10 days after the tragic accident, Margaret was asleep, or so she thought. Lying on her back with her eyes closed, she felt the unmistakable touch of a man's hand slipping underneath her neck. As her head was lifted

Fairy-Tale Love ♥

slightly off the pillow, she felt his gentle, loving kiss on her lips. After several seconds, he carefully lowered her head back to the pillow. The surreal encounter left her feeling like Sleeping Beauty being awakened from a deep slumber after the kiss of her true love. The entire ordeal left her with an enchanted, nostalgic happiness.

Encouraged by the sign Will had given her, Margaret's outlook improved. As she recounted the experience to her brother, she described the unique way her beloved husband had come to say his final good-bye. Her brother, however, had a different interpretation. He proposed that Will was actually saying hello rather than good-bye. Margaret was enchanted with that perspective and it fit her husband much better. How romantic a way to announce his presence to a wife he loved so very much.

That was the first of many communications Margaret and Will would share and one she would never forget. Compelled to preserve each experience she wrote a book, *No Regrets, My Love*. In this memoir, Margaret chronicles their life and journey together for the year following the loss. As it turns out, her romantic, fairy-tale marriage was not sacrificed by tragedy but rather grew stronger. Beyond the restrictions of earthly boundaries their love continues and like any good fairy tale...they live happily ever after.

~ Submitted by Margaret Cowie
Author of *No Regrets My Love*

Inspirational Stories
Multiple Submissions

For reasons that are unknown many have experienced not just one, but multiple ADCs. They consider these communications a blessing and perceive them as a continued bond with their departed loved one. These signs have served as proof to recipients that love and life are eternal.

A Pink Balloon, Please

Have you ever noticed how strict parents are with their first child? Being new to the game, they try to do everything just right and have high expectations for how their children should be. Then, with each additional child, the rules once applied slowly get pushed aside. When you are the youngest of multiple siblings, you pretty much have it made. Oftentimes, you end up getting babied much to the chagrin of the older siblings. Susan was not a spoiled child but she was the youngest of seven. Her mother was much more forgiving by the time Susan came into the picture.

For years, Susan had the opportunity to develop a very close bond with her mother. They had more than just a mother/daughter relationship. They were actually

♥ He Blew Her a Kiss

friends. Susan deeply respected her mother and regularly looked to her for advice. It was difficult for the entire family when the mother they loved so deeply was diagnosed with cancer. Susan spent countless hours with her mother as she fought a long and exhausting battle with an unforgiving disease. She admired her mother's fortitude but it was painful to see her as the disease slowly took over.

When her mother passed away on May 5, 2009, it proved to be an overwhelming burden upon Susan's soul. She knew for quite awhile that this day would come, but actually having to say good-bye was almost more than she could bear. The first few months following the funeral she fought the depression and sadness that frequently overcame her. So many times she simply could not stop the tears from streaming down her face.

One day she left work early in order to have lunch with her husband at his job. She found herself crying the entire way to pick up the food. Amidst the tears, she carried on a long conversation with her mother. Susan knew she was worrying excessively and didn't want to keep bothering her mother. She also knew that her mother should be left alone to enjoy her much deserved peace at last. However, she desperately needed some kind of sign that her mother was okay. She finally cried out, "Okay, Mama, just one pink balloon, not a bunch, just one." At the funeral, they had released pink balloons with white

A Pink Balloon, Please ♥

ribbons and she thought that would be a very appropriate sign.

Susan pulled into a BBQ place and ordered some food. After pulling off in the car, she realized she had forgotten drinks. She decided to stop at the gas station across the street, so she turned in and proceeded to pull into a space on the left. Before she could pull completely into her spot, she came to a dead stop. Right in front of her hovering close to the curb was a pink balloon with a white ribbon tied to it. Susan sat there in complete awe. Then she began to laugh and cry. In a loving voice, she told her mother she now knew for sure where she was and knew beyond a shadow of a doubt her mother was okay. All of a sudden the balloon was lifted by the wind and disappeared over the building. At that moment, Susan felt the huge burden that had been weighing her down disappear with the balloon. She immediately felt an immense peace that has remained with her to this day.

~ Submitted by Susan James

My Hero Forever

Susan lived what she considered to be a very normal life. She had a wonderful childhood growing up with six siblings and two loving parents. She counted herself fortunate when she met and married a very good man named Bob, who had two sons from a previous marriage. Having two children herself, they became one big happy family. Everything was going well up until she lost both parents to cancer. She felt the contentment from a full and satisfying life give way to a void that clouded her heart. Through it all she was forever thankful that her sisters and brothers were there for her. Sharing and relying on the love they had for one another helped ease the pain of their loss. As time went by they made adjustments and things began to take on a new kind of normalcy.

♥ He Blew Her a Kiss

It didn't surprise Susan that her older brother, Jim, became more and more of a father figure in the absence of their own. He had always been her hero and she looked up to him as much now as she did as a child. The pride she felt for him was deeply rooted. She fondly recalled a visit she had from him during the second grade. All the kids attended a Catholic school, and Jim being the second oldest had already graduated and joined the army. After completing basic training he came home and surprised her at school one day. She was so happy and proud he was there that at first she couldn't say a word. Beaming with excitement she finally declared to everyone around, "That's my big brother!" He immediately scooped her up and perched her atop his shoulders, carrying her all the way home.

As Susan grew up Jim was always there for her. He was there for the birth of her children and every other important event in her life, but she could count on him for the little things too. When Jim became a motorcycle police officer, Susan knew he would be very good at his job. He was already a hero in her eyes and such a giving and compassionate man. He was well respected by his colleagues, which spoke volumes of his character. Jim loved being a police officer and took great pride in his profession. Susan knew what he did was dangerous but she also knew how much it meant to him, so she faithfully prayed for his safety daily.

My Hero Forever ♥

On Sept 10, 2002, Susan was sitting at her desk at work. It was a beautiful day and her smile reflected her mood. The phone rang and she immediately recognized her aunt's voice on the other end. As her aunt quickly relayed what happened, Susan felt her good mood evaporate. One of her biggest fears had come to fruition. While on the job, Jim was involved in a serious accident. After teaching a class for the police department, he lost control of his motorcycle on the interstate and went into the grassy median. He hit a metal culvert and was thrown 50 feet. Her aunt told her he was alive but had been airlifted to the hospital in critical condition.

Susan left work frantically, worried about her brother. As tears threatened to spill forward she finally made it to the hospital. She parked and hurriedly rushed towards the entrance. Outside, police officers milled about, each one's face drawn pensively in concern. Brushing past the ocean of uniforms, she ran inside. After quickly learning where to find her brother, Susan stopped to take a deep breath. The doctor also informed her that Jim was in a coma and it was a very touchy situation. The outlook was grim but Susan refused to give up hope. Along with her sisters and brothers, they held diligent vigil over the brother they loved so much.

After several months they felt as if a miracle had occurred. Jim came out of his coma, conquering the first hurdle. Now he faced the daunting task of learning how to live all over again. Susan, who would have willingly given her own life for her brother, was fully prepared to help him with his rehabilitation. She was not alone, though; her other siblings did what they could as well. In fact they called themselves the A-team, stemming from their given last name of Ashe and the fact they were prepared to give it their all. It was challenging at times. It was incredibly hard to see Jim, who had always been such a strong and capable man, struggling with even the small tasks. At times he seemed as innocent and helpless as a child, and other times he was almost normal. Being a devout Catholic, Jim did not let his disabilities hinder his faith. He prayed the Rosary every day.

The traumatic brain injury he had sustained proved to be too much an obstacle for Jim to overcome. It was a heartbreaking day for Susan when he was moved from an assisted living facility to a nursing home. In some small way she felt as if they were admitting defeat and she still was not ready to call it quits. However, after going through the dying process with her parents, Susan sensed her brother was giving up. Every time she looked into his eyes, she saw the familiar look of discouragement and frustration she had seen not so long ago. She shared her observations with her siblings and they too had noticed how Jim was beginning to pull away from everyone. He had repeatedly told Susan that he didn't know what he would do without her. The truth is she didn't know what she was going to do without him.

Susan was hesitant to leave her brother's side, but her only daughter had given birth to her first baby girl. Even though she had five other grandchildren, Susan was quite anxious to be there for her daughter. Of course her sisters and brothers were close at hand to reassure her Jim would be well-cared for while she was gone. Still battling with mixed emotions, she decided to leave for Florida. Only one day after her arrival, she got the disturbing news that Jim had taken a turn for the worse. Susan was devastated and felt completely helpless being eight hours away. She begged her siblings to tell Jim she was on her way back and to please hold on.

The entire trip back Susan faced the difficult task of preparing herself for the worst. Still clinging to her faith, she prayed all the way back. Thankfully Jim was still holding on when she made it back. She rushed to her brother's side and took his hand into hers. His eyes were closed, but she knew in her heart he could hear every word as she whispered lovingly into his ear. She told him that everything was okay and he should get on his Harley and ride up into the clouds. She smiled and told him that Mama and Daddy would be right there waiting for him. She also reassured him that she would be okay. And with

♥ He Blew Her a Kiss

those words, a single tear rolled gently down Jim's face as he took his last breath. A mere 30 minutes had gone by from the time Susan arrived, and she was incredibly grateful that he had stayed with them long enough for her to relay her final words to him. It was September 11, 2009, seven years since his tragic accident. They all felt blessed to have had the additional time they were given with Jim.

Jim's funeral was wrought with emotion. The overwhelming number of people that came to pay their respects was testament to how much he was loved and respected. Susan along with her siblings found out so much about their older brother. They always knew that without fail they could count on Jim for anything at any time, but it was a little emotional to find out just how many people he had touched over his lifetime. One such individual had come forward while Jim had been in intensive care in a coma. She shared with them that she was a neighbor of his and that her house had burned down. Jim was so compassionate and caring that he had brought her and her family dinner almost every day until they could get things back in order. He was a sincere and genuine friend to everyone he knew.

Weeks later as Susan made her way home from work, her thoughts were on Jim. She still struggled with her loss and the tears flowed regularly. She fervently wished he

My Hero Forever

was right there with her. This was too much like losing her father all over again. Arriving at her house, she instinctively punched the garage door opener. Her eyes stared blankly as the door began to rise in front of her. All of a sudden she spotted someone in the garage. The door reached its highest point and revealed her brother Jim, standing right in front of her, dressed in his police uniform with his foot propped on her husband's four-wheeler. Susan felt her breath stop. She couldn't believe what she was seeing. Her eyes blinked and he was gone. It was a brief moment but she knew her brother was there letting her know that he was okay and that he would always be with her. Jim lifted her heart in one amazing moment. Not a day goes by that she doesn't think of him and all that he went through. However, from that point on she was able to release some of the pain, reassured that he was never far away.

~ Submitted by Susan James

Love Reflected in a Poem

Renee's father was born on July 22, 1926. Originally given the birth name Angelo Cavallo, he chose to go by his chosen patron saint name of James after his confirmation. However, friends and family just called him Jim. Being Italian, he was immersed in the concept that family was everything. He carried those beliefs with him when he became a father and had his own little family. Jim never completed high school, but he had a strong work ethic and was determined to make it on his own. Taking on any odd jobs that were available, he eventually settled into the workforce as a salesman. He dedicated himself to saving money in preparation for the family he knew would someday come.

Over time, Jim met many people but one person in particular, a woman named Katie, would prove to be very

♥ He Blew Her a Kiss

significant. Jim met Katie when she was married to her first husband. But Katie was someone you just couldn't forget. Very down to earth and real, it was hard not to like her. She kept a positive attitude and always tried to find the best in everything. They became friends but nothing more. It wasn't until Katie became pregnant with her first child that things would change. Her husband divorced and left her before their child was born and she felt completely alone. When it was time for her to give birth, she caught a bus to get to the hospital. Jim, being a friend, showed up for emotional support. Their bond continued to grow after that.

After her son was born, Katie applied to nursing school and Jim joined the army, ultimately leaving the country for Germany. After serving his time and returning home, he realized how much Katie meant to him. Having a strong bond and caring deeply for one another, they decided it was time to marry. Now Jim was responsible for his wife and her five-year-old son Ray. Although Ray was not his biological son, he treated him as if he was. Jim took wonderful care of his new family. After a year of marriage, they had their first child together, a daughter they named Renee. Girls are always near and dear to a father's heart and their case was no different. Renee was now and would forever be Daddy's little girl.

Love Reflected in a Poem ♥

Renee had very fond memories of growing up. Her father taught himself how to play the trumpet and had a deep love for Big Band music. These melodious sounds filled their home, giving Renee an appreciation of music as well. Sundays were family day, and after the kids got home from Mass they would all spend the day cleaning house, mowing the lawn, and washing the car. Jim made cooking spaghetti every Sunday a production. Being a very frugal man, no leftovers in the fridge were safe. Anything and everything found its way into the spaghetti. The kids always had a great laugh from trying to identify the variety of ingredients. Life was difficult for Jim and Katie, but they diligently trod along doing the best they could on a daily basis for their family.

Renee was in her early teens when her father was diagnosed with diabetes. He was advised by his doctor to work on his diet to help control it. At 40 years old, he tried to manage his weight but it seemed to be a losing battle. Arthritis had begun to creep in as well, making it harder for him to walk, exercise, or even get around like he had once done. For a man that was used to working hard every day of his adult life, just managing the simple things was taking its toll on his emotional well-being. Jim ended up having to retire, which only increased his frustration. His relationship with his wife Katie also had become strained, eventually ending up in divorce.

♥ He Blew Her a Kiss

After Renee turned 18, she married and moved out of her childhood home. She was happy with her new husband and things were going well for her. She kept in touch with her parents, however, and a close eye on her father's health. As his physical condition continued to decline, it became apparent things were not going to get any better. They were further disheartened when Jim was diagnosed with liver cancer in July 2007. His failing health made it necessary for Renee to take a leave of absence from her job in order to care for him along with the assistance of other family members. She didn't resent the additional responsibility she now faced because she loved her father very much. She stayed close to both her parents, keeping a closer vigilance on her father's health as he grew older.

Renee appreciated the time she was able to spend with her dad. Even though he was getting worse physically, his mind was still quite sharp. One thing he still enjoyed doing was crossword puzzles, and he would work six or seven of them a day. Having so much time together, Renee and her father spent many hours in conversation. Death was not an unusual topic for them to discuss. Renee lovingly listened to her father appreciating his attempt to prepare her for what would inevitably come. The only contribution she really had was to insist he somehow find a way to let her know he was okay. Some sort of sign, something

Love Reflected in a Poem ♥

she would know was only from him. She also strongly encouraged him to do the same for his sister, her Aunt Margaret.

One of Jim's wishes was to die at home. The family tried to honor his wishes and took care of him as long as they were able to, but his condition declined to the point it was necessary to admit him to the hospital. That was on Dec. 5, 2007, and sadly he was gone the very next day. It was a sorrowful loss for all who knew him. Family had meant the world to Jim his entire life, and he had proven to be a loving, inspirational, and supportive father. Being aware of his terminal condition, Renee was blessed to share what remaining time her father had left, demonstrating how much she really loved him.

The day after her father died, Renee made her way into the salon she had been a patron of for years to have her hair done. She walked directly over to her hairdresser and threw her purse and keys onto the station across from her chair. They came to rest against the mirror more than a foot from the edge of the counter. Renee took a seat and began discussing what she wanted done. Suddenly, her keys seemed to have a life of their own and jumped completely off the counter onto the floor. She sat there in amazement staring at her keys. There was no possible way they just fell off. The many conversations she and her father shared immediately came to mind and she

131

♥ He Blew Her a Kiss

truly believed this incident was a sign from her father letting her know he was still around. Little did she know this would not be the only time she would feel her father's presence.

The day after her father's funeral, Renee was feeling a little lost. For a while now, all her spare time and energy had gone to caring for her father and now he was gone. Taking the first step in readjusting her time, she climbed the stairs and entered what she called her junk room. Now was as good a time as any to work on straightening up. Her attention fell on a stack of papers that had been sitting there for months. When she picked it up, a single piece fell to the floor. Renee reached down to retrieve it when she noticed the writing. It was a poem entitled "A Message from Heaven."

> Perhaps you aren't ready yet
> to have to say goodbye...
> Perhaps you've thought of things
> you wish you'd said—well, so have I.
> For one thing, I'd have told you
> not to worry about me...
> I'm with the Lord in Heaven now—
> you knew that's where I'd be.
> I'm sorry that you're feeling sad
> for I'm so happy now.

Love Reflected in a Poem ♥

I've asked the Lord to ease the hurt
and comfort you somehow.
It's hard at the beginning
but I know you'll make it through.
I hope it helps to know
that I'll be waiting here for you.

– Author Unknown

When Renee read those words, her knees buckled and she collapsed to the floor. Although it brought tears instantly, they were tears of joy and comfort, not of pain. What a special way for her father to convey his message of love. She gently thanked him for granting her wish of reassurance. At that moment, she realized how beneficial her talks with her father had been. Even though it had been difficult to discuss death, especially with a parent, the result had provided an immeasurable sense of peace and comfort. Asking for a sign may have seemed a little uncomfortable at first, but she was glad she had asked. Renee could move forward in her own life with the reassurance that all was well with her father.

~ Submitted by Renee Taber

I Can Always Count on Mom

As Katie watched the cars go by, she attempted to remain relatively calm. Even though she was in a great deal of pain, she recognized the sheer determination that had come to her aid all her life and it was kicking into full throttle. Her husband had left her alone and pregnant and her child was ready to be born regardless of the situation. She stood as the bus approached, praying she would make it on time. After maneuvering into a seat, she tried to relax even if it was only briefly. Her contractions were becoming closer and closer. In spite of her strength and independence, Katie longed for her mother's guidance and reassurance. She barely remembered her mother since she had lost her at such a young age, but she instinctively knew how big a difference it would have

♥ He Blew Her a Kiss

made to have her here. She battled against the cramped space and once again rose to her feet. Thankfully this was her stop.

Katie gave birth to a healthy baby boy and named him Ray. As soon as she cradled him in her arms, nothing else mattered. No matter what, she would never be alone again. The love between mother and child was nearly tangible. She didn't have any family there to welcome Ray into the world, but her friend Jim did show up. He came as soon as he found out, and was eager to be a supportive friend. Jim and Katie had been friends, and he cared very much about her welfare. He felt compelled by his affection for her to take care of them as best he could. When Katie left the hospital, she had her son in her arms and Jim by her side. Thankful for the extra moral and emotional support, she was confident everything was going to be just fine.

Jim kept his promise and continued to be there. Ray was growing by leaps and bounds and Katie proved to be a wonderful mother. She adored her son and Jim had proven to be an answered prayer. As circumstances would have it though, Jim joined the army and was sent to Germany. While he was gone, Katie took the opportunity to better her chances for the future. She enrolled in nursing school and found she was quite adept at it. Excelling to the top of the class, she was both proud and

I Can Always Count on Mom ♥

excited. However, since she had never graduated from high school, the nursing school would not allow her to continue.

Katie was a determined individual though, and was not going to allow anyone to hold her back. She applied for jobs, and one application in particular asked if she could type. Although she couldn't, she didn't hesitate to mark "yes." Promptly leaving the job interview, she went straight to the store, bought a typewriter, got a book, and learned that very weekend how to type. Her dedication paid off because the following week she got the job. She continued working even after Jim returned from Germany. They decided to get married in 1952, and in 1953 had their daughter, Renee. It wasn't long before they welcomed a third child into the family, a healthy baby boy named Vince.

Katie soon discovered she was pregnant again and elated with the news. Then the doctor threw her a curve ball that was totally unexpected. She was carrying twins. Initially the news overwhelmed her, but she quickly embraced the concept and eagerly awaited their arrival. She gave birth to boys, Michael and Steven, but tragically, they both passed only a few days later. She was devastated beyond belief. As a mother, the bond had already developed during the time she carried them, and losing them broke her heart. She became engulfed in a sea of

♥ He Blew Her a Kiss

sadness, and no words of encouragement could stem the flow of tears that marked this dark time in her life.

Although the loss was difficult for Katie, she wasn't one to shirk responsibilities. Pulling herself together for her children's sake, she pushed the depression deep into her soul and moved forward. The opportunity came up for her to get in on the ground floor at Campbell Clinic when it opened. Jumping at the chance, she threw herself into the job as a surgical nurse in orthopedics and had no regrets. With positive determination, she handled being a professional and a mother, maintaining a healthy balance between the two. With a sense of pride and accomplishment, she watched her children grow into adulthood. However, the time had come when she and Jim decided it best to part ways, and in 1974 they divorced.

Three years later Katie met Raymond Nelson. He was a WWII vet and their friendship grew. They discovered they had a great deal in common and in 1977 she married him. Together they had a home built in Crenshaw, Miss., and named it "Honeysuckle Hill." Katie retired from St. Jude, where she was employed as an EEG technician, to enjoy her new home in the country. The house was built on a large amount of land where they planted and grew things. They loved animals, especially dogs, and they had plenty of room to have a few. Looking back on her life, Katie appreciated every step that had led her to this point.

I Can Always Count on Mom ♥

She may have had a difficult childhood, but she chose to see the good in people and turn negative situations into positive ones. At last, she was rewarded with a peaceful contentment she richly deserved.

Sadly, Katie's world changed when she began suffering from Alzheimer's, which is a particularly difficult disease for which loved ones have to deal. Because of its nature and the way it affects a patient, comforting trips down memory lane are no longer possible. Patients often don't recognize the ones they love, making it difficult to act on emotional bonds that have been nurtured over years. Katie made many friends during her lifetime and she had family that loved her dearly. When it all ended on Aug. 16, 2008, many people mourned her loss, especially her children.

For Renee in particular, losing her mother was very difficult. Katie had always been such a positive and nurturing influence on her. She had already lost her father. Now the only parent she had left was gone as well. Renee felt a void that even with time would be difficult to heal. Having three children of her own, she knew life must continue on, and she faced it one day at a time. She stayed busy with work and her children and, before she knew it, more than a year had passed.

It was Thanksgiving night 2009, and Buddy, an 11-year-old pit bull terrier, had fallen ill. He had been

♥ He Blew Her a Kiss

with the family a long time and was like another child to Renee. Watching him get progressively worse, she frantically called around searching for a vet, but everyone was closed because of the holiday. Finally she located one that was open and took him there. She had no choice but to leave him in their care. Trying to remain optimistic, Renee hoped Buddy would return home on Saturday.

Much to her disappointment the vet called Saturday and said that Buddy had begun having seizures. His condition had progressed to the point they would have to make a quality-of-life decision for him. Sadness filled the house when Renee explained what was going on to her kids. She then quietly said a prayer to her mother. Katie and Buddy had been best of friends while she was alive and she truly loved him. Renee felt it very appropriate to ask her mother to please come and take Buddy home to Heaven so he wouldn't suffer any more. She didn't want to have to make the decision to put him to sleep. As they were preparing to leave, the vet called and told her Buddy had passed away. Renee quietly thanked her mom for answering her prayer. She then told the vet they wanted to come and get him so they could bury him at home.

The family climbed into the car with heads hung low and tears in their eyes. They retrieved their beloved Buddy and brought him back to the house. It was cold

I Can Always Count on Mom ♥

outside and Renee's son was going to dig the grave. He got the shovel and went around to the back gate, forgetting it was padlocked. He came back in the house and told his mother he needed the key. However, it had been moved from its usual place. Everyone began searching for it. Renee's daughter Jennifer opened up the box her mother kept in the dining room. She searched inside and found a pair of green rosary beads Katie had given to Renee, and a few other things, but no key. She closed the box and put it back where she had found it. Finally the key was located and they proceeded with Buddy's burial.

Afterwards, everyone was sitting at the kitchen table talking and Renee noticed her green rosary beads sitting on the counter next to the microwave. She asked her children if one of them had left the beads sitting there. Everyone replied "no." Jennifer spoke up and told her she had seen them in the box when she was looking for the key but she never took them out. That's when her daughter-in-law spoke up, "Maybe it's divine intervention." All Renee could do was smile and nod in agreement. She knew in her heart her mother had been there. The rosary beads held a strong emotional tie to her mother, and that's why she believed Katie used them to convey the simple message to her that Buddy was safe, secure, and happy.

Although it was difficult for Renee to say good-bye to a pet that was more like a child to her, it eased her pain

♥ He Blew Her a Kiss

knowing that he was in the capable hands of someone that loved him as much as she did. Even though she already missed Buddy, she was thankful he was not alone. For Renee, there could be no other explanation for how those beads moved from inside the box to the countertop without assistance from anyone else in the house. The sign itself was amazing, but the most significant thing she gained was the knowledge that her mother was still close by. Renee felt she had lost her mother forever when she passed away. Now she knew Katie was aware of everything going on in her life and was relieved to have her mother's love so near.

~ Submitted by Renee Taber

Wings of Love

Sheila woke up to a breathtaking array of pink and blue as the sun peeked over the eastern horizon. In their home, the entire family was early to rise. Time was not to be wasted. If she hurried, she might just catch her father before he left for work. His job at the farm kept him away from home from sunup to sundown. She got to the door just as he was about to open it and looked up, waiting. He paused and looked down at her with complete adoration. He bent over and wrapped his strong sun-baked arms around her waist as she planted her morning kiss on his cheek. Sheila said good-bye and he walked out the door.

A familiar sound from the kitchen caught her attention. She peeked around the corner just as Mom put breakfast

♥ He Blew Her a Kiss

on the table. By this time, her two younger brothers, Stan and Mark, had joined them as her mother called out for the two oldest to come on. When Rubin and Roy made it into the kitchen, they sat down together and ate their meager breakfast as if it were a feast. Afterwards, Mom did the dishes as all the children got dressed.

Sheila's mother, Lottie B., worked just as hard to provide for her family. Her dedication to her husband and her children set an incredible example, especially for her young daughter. Sheila could even recall her mother pulling her behind on a cotton sack as she chopped and picked cotton in the fields. Even with her mother working to help her father, money was still scarce. However, her parents made sure the children never went without.

The most exciting time for them came at Christmas. Sneaking into their parents' room, the children were overwhelmed with the scent of fresh fruit. Waiting the two weeks until Christmas Day kept the house filled with excitement. Finally, on that special morning each child would awaken to their own paper grocery sack that contained an orange, an apple, and lots of nuts. There was also one present apiece. It was a happy and joyful family that celebrated Christmas together, thankful for what they had.

As Sheila grew up, she realized that even though they always had clothes to wear, shoes on their feet, and school supplies they needed, her parents had oftentimes gone without. Knowing the sacrifices her parents endured made her love and appreciate them that much more. Sheila was thankful for her close, loving family.

Getting together throughout the years were times Sheila cherished. Family gatherings gave them the opportunity to look back and laugh at some of the silly antics they went through growing up. One story that always brought a chuckle was one that occurred when Sheila was only 12 years old. On that particular day, Rubin and Roy exited the house with a purpose. As they passed Sheila playing in the yard, they warned her, "Sister, we're goin' out in the woods and smoke us a cigarette. Don't tell Daddy where we went!" With that, they disappeared into the trees. It wasn't much later when her father came out of the house. He had been looking for the boys. He called to her, "Sister, do you know where the boys are?" Sheila innocently replied, "I can't tell you where they went but they went to smoke 'em a cigarette." Her daddy did an abrupt turnaround and strode back into the house. A moment later he emerged with a cane pole and a stern look on his face. He made his way into the woods as well. Needless to say the boys were quite mad at their sister for telling on them. She pleaded to the fact they didn't tell her not to say what they were doing. At the time, it wasn't very funny to the boys, but looking back they all

♥ He Blew Her a Kiss

got a good laugh at it. There were many similar stories that each time shared only strengthened their bond.

Stability and strength exemplified by their parents also served to strengthen the family bond. Never ones to complain, they showed there was much more to life than just material wealth. True wealth could be measured in the love they all shared for one another. Due to the fact their parents never complained, Sheila was alarmed when her mother revealed she had been having difficulty breathing. She knew it had to be serious because Lottie B. never complained. To complicate matters even more, she would get sick every time she tried to eat. Due to the lack of nourishment and her worsening ability to breathe, Lottie B. finally agreed to go to the doctor. They were devastated by the diagnosis that she had esophageal cancer. The only treatment offered was radiation. Sheila knew how hard this would be on her mother so she made a special effort to help as much as possible. Sometimes she would relieve her dad and take Mom in for the radiation. It broke her heart every time as she watched her mother climb up on the sterile, unforgiving table and quietly subject herself to the damaging treatment. Sheila longed to be able to hold her mother's hand, letting her know she was right there by her side through such an ordeal. Because of the radiation, though, she was only allowed to watch helplessly through an impersonal glass window.

After Lottie B. finished her round of radiation, her family was devoted to nursing her back to health. It was a slow process, but it was a labor of love. It was approximately three months later she began having a pain under her right breast. Still vigilant in the care of her mother, Sheila took her back to the doctor after a series of tests. So far their experience with the hospital to this point had been disappointing at best. This trip would prove to be no better. The news was deflating. The doctor began to share the diagnosis of liver cancer. At that point, Sheila's heart sank and her mind raced. She didn't even hear the rest of the doctor's conversation. She grasped desperately to the inner strength her mother had instilled inside her. Above all, she had to be strong for her mother and father through this. What started out as two sessions of chemo turned into multiple sessions without any hint of relief. If anything, her mother seemed to suffer more. Her weakness combined with unrelenting pain kept her mother sick and confined to bed. The family felt helpless. The best they could do was pray and be there for her. Lottie B. had begun praying. She spent many hours praying that God would mercifully take her out of her pain.

On Aug. 20, 2002, God answered Lottie B.'s prayers and brought her home. Sheila mourned the loss of her mother, but she felt equally sad for her father, David. Her parents had been together for so many years and she

♥ He Blew Her a Kiss

could see the loss reflected in his eyes. It was only a day after they had recognized David's birthday. It had not really been a celebration because of the serious condition Lottie B. had been in. Although many tears were shed as they took her mother away, Sheila silently thanked God that her mother was no longer in pain. Just as the second door was being closed on the van a large, beautiful butterfly emerged. It headed straight for her father and circled him over and over. David exclaimed, "Look at this!" as his eyes followed every move the butterfly made. With total conviction they all truly believed Lottie B. was saying her final good-bye. Her spirit was finally free to float on the wings of love.

~ Submitted by Sheila Bowman

Believe in Yourself

Sheila was getting increasingly frustrated. She felt as if everything was falling apart. After losing her husband Nick, nothing seemed to go right. The first thing to go in the house was the heat. Not long after that the air conditioner went out, not once, but twice. The patio door hinges locked up from lack of use, followed by the patio screens getting blown out from the weather. Why was all this happening now? Sheila wondered what she could have possibly done to deserve all this bad luck. Normally, Nick handled the "honey do" list with ease and things never seemed that bad.

With Nick gone now, Sheila had to face these problems alone and it was beginning to get a little overwhelming. She had never been handy with tools nor did she have

♥ He Blew Her a Kiss

any clue about how to fix anything. As daunting as these tasks were already, the list just seemed to get longer. One of the toilets in the house broke, and finally the refrigerator gasped its last breath. For three weeks, it felt as if she were camping, living completely out of a cooler. She tried desperately to salvage the food that had previously occupied the now useless refrigerator. Despite her efforts, she lost almost everything that had been frozen. Thank goodness a new one was scheduled to be delivered.

The next day Sheila tried to focus on work, but the long list of things to fix still nagged away at her. Feeling somewhat helpless, she headed home for the day. She pulled the car into the drive around 5:30 that evening and pushed the garage door opener. The car idled as she watched the door creeping upward. She eased up into her spot and once again punched the button. As the door lowered halfway down it jerked to a stop and then proceeded to rise back up. Sheila exclaimed, "What now?" She longed for her husband to be there and hopelessly looked upward and said, "Honey, you know what I need."

Almost instantly, it seemed as if Sheila was in a trance as she made her way towards Nick's toolbox. Poking around inside it, she finally pulled out a monkey wrench and walked over to the ladder. Once it was in position, she climbed up. With unfamiliar confidence, she began

Believe in Yourself ♥

working on the garage door. As she loosened and removed a part, the cable fell down to the ground and all she could do was laugh about it. Reality suddenly hit her. What on earth did she think she was doing? About to give up, Sheila heard Nick's voice as he simply told her, "Just let it go and don't worry." She knew then that Nick was somehow guiding her through this. Rather than giving up, she proceeded to work on the door, truly not knowing what she was doing. Before long it was fixed!

Well aware of her own ineptitude when it came to anything mechanical, Sheila was bewildered at what she had just accomplished. Things like this just didn't happen. She felt in some way it had to be credited to Nick. She didn't know how, nor could she explain it, but somehow he had guided her into doing what needed to be done. Tears nearly overcame her as she thought about how he had always been there for her. She truly believed that he still had her back. In truth, Sheila felt a new invigorating faith that she could overcome anything. With relatively few complaints, Nick handled his "honey do" lists like a pro. Now it was time for Sheila to step up to the plate. He had given her the reassurance and encouragement she needed to believe in herself. In his own way, Nick had shown her that she could do anything. Knowing that her beloved husband was in her corner left her feeling blessed and loved.

~ Submitted by Sheila Bowman

Never Far Away

Have you ever known someone that has endured extreme mishaps in their life? Susan's father, Alex, was just such a person. His childhood through adult life was filled with one mishap after another, and yet he still survived to marry and have children. Susan learned her father's past was quite interesting growing up as a young lad in Toronto, Canada. His family, in keeping with his Scottish ancestors, made their living as haberdashers and tinkers. They did not live in permanent dwellings. Instead they traveled from town to town in wagons selling homemade pots and pans during the day and setting up camp at night. The women would sell ribbon and lace in addition to needles, thread, and other sewing utensils. The Williamson men provided for the family as well by breeding and selling horses. Although Alex's father did not have horses, the honor of being chosen by Queen Victoria to provide all her white horses was bestowed to his relatives. They did not sell them to her, but rather loaned them with the understanding they would be returned after their time of service instead of being put down. It was a tough and meager, yet honest existence that in turn made their families strong.

Susan learned about some of their family tree after talking with a cousin. He recounted stories about his Uncle Alex his own mother shared with him before she died. His mother, Alex's sister, admitted she was shocked her brother had survived his youth. It was obvious he either possessed a strong will to live or he was a very fortunate person. Her list of ailments and/or events he survived was amazing. By age six, he had overcome pleurisy, had pulled a pot of boiling water off the stove onto himself, had been hit by a streetcar, and survived being run over by a truck. In 1939, he joined the Canadian army and served under Montgomery in the first company that landed in Sicily during World War II. During a battle, Alex took six bullets in the stomach. The pain seared through his gut like a hot knife and he dove into the nearest trench. But in so doing, he broke his neck. Miraculously his spinal cord was not severed. Covered with a sheet and left for dead, he lay helpless for 17 hours before someone discovered he was still alive. He was rushed into surgery, where they removed 75 percent of his stomach.

Alex was like a cat with nine lives, and even after the war he found no respite from mishaps. While working in a factory he was run over by a forklift, resulting in two broken legs. Then, in 1960, it was discovered that phosphorus from the bullets he had taken during the war had slowly eaten away at his spine, forcing him to undergo a spinal fusion. A second spinal surgery was required later and this procedure left his legs numb. He was told he would never walk again. Alex was not one to give up, though. A year later, he was walking with a cane, a clear testament to his indomitable spirit. With that victory Alex shared his plans to live to 100, and from his track record of beating the odds everyone thought he just might do it.

In relation to everything that had happened so far, Alex had what could be considered an uneventful span. He did develop diabetes but was controlling that fairly well. Then one morning he awoke and headed into the bathroom to wash up. He had what he called a dizzy spell and fell. Susan received a phone call her father was in the hospital. When she got there, he was still in the emergency room. That's when she discovered he had hit his head in the fall, which in turn knocked him unconscious. He endured test after test when they finally determined he had suffered a mild stroke. He seemed to be recovering

♥ He Blew Her a Kiss

fairly well but had to stay in the hospital, at least for the night.

The next day Susan was distressed to hear Alex was taking a turn for the worse. The doctors were concerned because his body was beginning to shut down. They advised her to make any calls she felt were necessary. Of course, she contacted her brother Scott, who lived in Vancouver. He immediately got on a plane. Once he arrived, he joined Susan and his mother at the hospital. All three were there when Alex began having seizures the following day. There was nothing the doctors could do to improve his condition so they gave him Valium to ease his pain and make him more comfortable. It was difficult for Susan to admit, but it was painfully apparent that he was not going to survive much longer.

Later that evening Susan was sitting with her father. At exactly 7 p.m., she looked at him and instinctively knew he had just drawn his last breath. Refusing to let him go, she ran out of the room calling for help. Frantic and somewhat angry for the prolonged lack of response, she began crying. She knew her father had a "do not resuscitate" order but she didn't care. She wanted so desperately for him to stay with her. She didn't want to believe this was really happening. Her mother and brother urged her to calm down, but when she let go of the anger and frustration she just started feeling numb. They decided to give her a little more time alone in the room. As she sat there helpless, an odd thought suddenly crossed her mind. She hadn't yet repaid the 40 dollars she'd recently borrowed from her dad. All she could do was keep apologizing and insisting one day she would pay him back. She finally left his room and rejoined her family, feeling a large void in that place in her heart she held especially for him.

After her father's passing, Susan continued to struggle with her loss. Roughly two years had gone by and she still missed him terribly. One night after getting home from her job on the subway at three a.m., she could hardly wait to crawl into bed. She quickly changed into her nightclothes and slipped under the covers. Almost instantly upon nestling her head into the pillow, she felt the bed shake as if someone had bumped into it. Before she could even react, it felt like someone actually sat down on the end of the bed at her feet. Immediately Susan was taken aback by what was happening. Her first thought was that she was having a nervous breakdown or maybe she was just too exhausted. Even though she had not seen anyone, she jumped up and checked her apartment to make sure it had not been broken into. All the doors and windows were locked, verifying she was the only one there. Although a little apprehensive, she knew she had to get some rest and eventually fell asleep.

At work the following day, Susan had time to think about what had happened. Ruling out a nervous breakdown, she had a small inkling of what it could have been. When she arrived home and went to bed, the exact same thing happened again like a surreal sense of déjà vu. This time, however, she was not caught off guard. She was prepared and much less afraid. Acting on her own beliefs regarding the source, Susan directed her question towards the end of the bed. "Dad, is that you?" Of course, there was no verbal response but she knew it was him. She could sense his presence close to her. With an audible sigh of relief she said, "I'm glad you came to see me. It makes me feel much better." Suddenly the void she had carried since his death seemed to fade as comfort and happiness took its place. Susan drifted off to sleep and enjoyed the best rest she had experienced during the entire past year.

Alex's visits were not limited to just those first two nights. He continued to visit Susan every night for more than two years. During this time, she began coping better with the loss of her father and her daily routine seemed much less burdened. God often balances the loss of one family member with the birth of a new one, and Susan was soon to welcome a grandchild. In 2001, four years after Alex passed, her daughter Natalie gave birth to a healthy baby boy she named Hunter. When Hunter was a month old, Susan went to stay with her daughter for a few months to help out with the new addition. During her visit, they noticed that when Hunter was being held his eyes would become fixed on something no one else could see. They would deliberately position themselves in his direct line of sight but he always seemed to look past them in the distance just above them. He would laugh and giggle as if he were watching someone. Susan believed her father, who loved children and was always trying to make them giggle and laugh, was there watching over them. He had a special bond with Natalie and she too believed it was her Grampy Alex as well, admiring his great-grandson. It made Susan happy to think Natalie and Hunter had an extra guardian angel looking out for them.

When Susan returned home from her visit, she felt all was well with her family, and her newfound peace was reflected in the smile on her face. As she prepared for bed that first night back, her thoughts returned to her own experiences with her father and she was thankful for his love. Climbing into bed she was pleasantly surprised to feel it bump again just like before. All she could do was smile and drift to sleep with happy thoughts filling her head. Strangely, it never happened again after that night, which was disappointing for Susan because she wanted the visits to last forever. Looking back though, she knew her father was confirming his love for her and saying his final good-bye until they were together again.

♥ He Blew Her a Kiss

It was a long time before Susan ever shared her experiences with anyone. She was afraid others would think she was crazy. That's why, one day during a conversation with her brother Scott, she understood his concern. It was obvious he wanted to share something with her but was somewhat hesitant. He said, "I had the strangest thing happen to me, Sister. I don't know if I should tell you, you'll think I'm nuts." Before he could even finish, Susan reassured him and told him she had something to share with him too. Scott proceeded to tell her that one night as he prepared for bed, from out of nowhere he clearly heard his father call out his name. It literally made him swing around fully expecting to see his dad standing behind him. He said it was so real he truly thought he was in the room with him. Susan nodded, fully understanding what had happened. She told Scott she too had gone through something similar and proceeded to share her story with him.

At first, both Susan and Scott worried about what other people would think but quickly realized that they were fortunate, not crazy. Most people do not realize how often these types of communications occur. It doesn't happen to everyone, but it happens to many and there's no apparent criteria you have to meet to experience an after-death communication, or ADC. People from all walks of life, from different religious affiliations and from different races, can experience an ADC. Spiritual encounters cannot be forced or predicted. It may not happen right away. Our loved ones can communicate at any time. It might be very soon after their transition, or it could be months or even years later. People can only remain open to the possibilities. Above all, don't be afraid or think that you are going crazy. Communications are a blessing and are truly treasured by people that understand our loved ones are only lost physically. Spiritually they are always with us. Susan took great comfort from her father's visits, and just the reassurance it provided helped her realize that she would one day see him again.

~ Submitted by Susan Williamson

The Beauty of a Butterfly

Susan had already gone through the pain of losing her father eight years earlier. Now, as if that wasn't enough, she faced the devastating news that her mother, Gerry, had ovarian cancer. Her father had shown her through a series of after-death communications that death was not the end. Yet, she was still not prepared to let go of her only surviving parent. Growing up, Susan and her father had shared a special bond, while her brother Scott seemed closer to their mother. She knew without a doubt that her father was proud of her and approved of how her life had turned out, but she wasn't as sure her mother shared that belief. Now was Susan's opportunity to step up to the plate and show her mother she was there for her. She loved her mother and wanted to do her best

♥ He Blew Her a Kiss

for her, especially now, when her mother needed her the most.

Gerry moved in with Susan after she was diagnosed. The cancer had not been detected until it was already in stage three. The doctors were unable to give her any kind of accurate estimate on the time she had left. Her own body, and how it handled the chemo treatments, would determine that. Not knowing, they felt it would be best if she came to live with Susan. Gerry was adamant about not wanting to die at a hospital so she made Susan promise not to take her, no matter what. Her mother fought valiantly against the cancer, and for three more years they had an opportunity to nurture the bond between them. Seeing her mother's courage gave Susan a newfound appreciation and a deeper love for the woman that had raised her and meant so much to her.

In March 2005, Susan and her mother were advised by the oncologists to go ahead and make final preparations. They contacted the funeral home and asked for a representative to come to the house. Gerry was able to make her own decisions and pick out everything so it would be exactly how she wanted it. She decided to be cremated just as her husband had been, so she picked out a beautiful brass enamel urn. It had delicate butterflies on it with one white butterfly that prominently stood out.

The Beauty of a Butterfly ♥

Satisfied with her choices, she felt it was one less burden for which her children would have to deal.

Since losing her husband, Gerry had felt so alone. They had been married close to 58 years. During the last month of her life, she became weary and tired of the struggle. All the arrangements had been made and there was really nothing left for her to do. Although she loved her children dearly, she was ready to finally reunite with her husband Alex. Twice she told her daughter that she wished God would go ahead and take her. She just didn't want to fight any longer. Having experienced the comforting presence of her father after he died, Susan felt compelled to make a final request of her mother. She chose a quiet moment and said, "Mom, if you can come back, will you?" Her mother never answered the question. Instead she was just staring up into the corner of the room. Susan asked her, "Are you all right, Mom?" She was becoming a little scared until her mother smiled and said, "Doesn't he have lovely blue eyes?" Somewhat relieved, Susan immediately thought of her father. He had jet black hair and gorgeous blue eyes. She quickly asked, "Who, Mom?" Her mother still didn't answer but Susan felt her father was close by waiting to take his wife home.

A couple of days later, Gerry became very restless. She was having trouble breathing so Susan said, "Mom, you've got to relax because you're making yourself panic

♥ He Blew Her a Kiss

and that's why it's hard for you to breath." Honoring the promise she'd made to her mother, Susan resisted the urge to rush her to the hospital. Instead, she called the doctor and was advised to give her mother a pill that would help calm her down. After her mother settled down a bit, Susan felt completely drained. It was out of character for her to want to go to sleep this early, but she felt an uncanny necessity to do so. Susan settled onto the couch next to her mother's bed. At her mother's request, the lights were left on but she found herself unable to fall asleep with them shining in her face. Pulling the covers over her head she finally drifted off.

Because Susan had somehow sensed an urgency to go to sleep that evening, she was spared the agony of watching another parent die in front of her eyes. Instead, Susan awoke to discover her mother had passed quietly during the night. With a heavy heart, she made the phone call to the funeral home. About two hours after they left, she made her way outside to sit on the back steps of her apartment. Susan lived in downtown Toronto and ever since she and her mother had moved in, the back steps had served as a retreat to escape for a quick prayer and time to think. Looking over the parking lot and mourning the loss of her mother, she wondered if she had done the right thing in her mother's eyes. Had she pleased her mother enough? Her approval meant so much to Susan.

The Beauty of a Butterfly ♥

Her heart somehow needed that confirmation. She continued sitting there looking out at the cars parked in her backyard—"the asphalt jungle," as she called it.

Suddenly a white butterfly fluttered up right in front of her face. Its fragile wings carried it back and forth as if it wanted to land on her. During the 20 years she had lived there, she had never seen a butterfly anywhere around. There were no flowers or anything there that would even remotely attract a butterfly. She quickly concluded this had to be a sign from her mother. The beautiful urn her mother had picked out immediately came to mind as the biggest butterfly on the urn was a white one. Susan instantly filled with excitement and said, "You must be Mom. This is the sign I wanted." For an entire week, every time she went outside this same white butterfly would come to her. Susan believed this sign was actual confirmation from her mother that she did approve of the daughter she had raised. With that realization, the daily visits from the butterfly ceased.

Susan's mother was cremated and the funeral went exactly as she had planned except for one thing. Gerry had instructed the family to bury her ashes alongside her husband's ashes. Susan just could not bring herself to bury them yet. So until she was ready, they stayed with her on the bookcase in the living room along with their pictures. Every day she would talk to them and every

♥ He Blew Her a Kiss

evening she told them good-night. Whenever she had a problem, she would talk to them about it. Some people might not understand just having them there was very comforting. She fully intended to abide by her mother's wishes, but for now she felt better with them there.

Almost three years had gone by before Susan finally felt she could let go and bury her mother and father's ashes in the family plot. She began making preparations for the ceremony. Both parents had served as privates in the Canadian army, so she had a military headstone made for them. Her mother had often shared with her that some of her happiest years were in the army. She loved the group The Moody Blues as well, so Susan chose two of their songs, "I Know You're Out There Somewhere" and "Tuesday Afternoon," which was Gerry's favorite. Another song, "Company B" by the Andrews Sisters, also was played in honor of her husband's company during WWII. To honor her father's Scottish heritage, she secured a bagpipe player to perform "Amazing Grace." And finally, she had a military padre to lead the service.

The night before the internment, Susan wanted to make her last evening with her parents a special one. She put in a movie they loved, set their urns next to her on the couch, and curled up under a blanket and watched it. It seemed to be a fitting conclusion to her time with her parents that was very comforting and helped bring closure.

The Beauty of a Butterfly ♥

The following day the ceremony proved to be quite moving. There were approximately 20 people in attendance, and she felt her parents would have been very moved and honored at the outpouring of love for them. Afterwards, her family went out to eat. Her cousins Sue and Margaret were there, buzzing with excitement. Both of them blurted out, "Did you see that white butterfly that was there during the service? It went to each and every one of us." Susan had indeed noticed it, but did not realize the significance until that moment. It had been more than three years ago when she had first been visited by a white butterfly. Once she made the connection, she realized her parents had been there in spirit after all. To her, the butterfly signified her parents were together and happy and they were definitely aware of what was occurring in the lives of the loved ones they had left behind.

~ Submitted by Susan Williamson

The Right Choice

As Kimberly sat in the chair between her husband and her father, she was completely numb. She could hear the words as the funeral director spoke. She could see his lips moving but nothing seemed to register in her mind. The whole situation was like a horrible dream that she couldn't wake up from. Even something as simple as breathing was difficult. In the past twenty-four hours, life as they knew it had ceased to exist.

Without prompting, her thoughts rushed back to the day their oldest daughter, Elizabeth, was preparing to leave home and attend college at the University of Minnesota. In spite of her mixed emotions about her firstborn leaving the nest, Kimberly and her husband Roger were very proud of their daughter. She had enjoyed helping Liz gather up everything needed to move out on her own, even though she knew how much she would miss her. Her daughter was so excited to be spreading her wings and venturing out into a new life of true independence. Finally the day arrived and she was off to face the world.

Liz did well in school, and before they knew it a year had already passed. Prior to beginning her sophomore year, she and a few friends decided to move into a duplex that was only a few blocks from campus. Then tragedy struck. Kimberly and Roger received the call that all parents fear. Much to their horror they were informed that a fire had broken out at the duplex. Liz and two of her roommates had died from smoke inhalation. Devastated, Kimberly barely remembered anything that happened after that.

Her mind crashed back to the present as the funeral director's voice interrupted her reminiscing. He asked question after question that she had no choice but to answer. What was her birth date? Where was she born? What year did she graduate from high school? Kimberly answered them all without any thought. At that moment she felt more like a robot, emotionally void, than a mother. Part of her wished she could just run out of the room screaming. She wanted to run home and find her beautiful daughter safe and sound in her room. She could picture Liz with a coy smile on her face telling her, "Oh

Mom, you just worry way too much! Nothing is going to happen to me! I'm just fine!"

Why couldn't this all be just a horrible nightmare, or some cruel joke? Please God, please. Liz was only 20 years old. It was incomprehensible that she was gone. Kimberly knew that denial was useless. This was reality and she had to accept it and learn to live again. As the funeral director left the room briefly, they sat there like statues staring blankly into space. Conversation was impossible and the silence in the room was deafening. They were clinging to a fine line of keeping their composure when her husband dropped his head into his hands and sobbed. With a sense of urgency he stood up and hurried out of the room. Stifling his tears he mumbled the fact that he had to get some air. Barely acknowledging him, Kimberly and her father sat in their chairs as the tears streamed down their faces. When the funeral director returned, he gently informed them that they would need to provide clothes for Liz to be buried in. As his words slowly sank in, Kimberly mentally scanned her daughter's closet at the house and realized there was nothing left. She had taken all her clothes with her to school.

Facing the difficult task ahead, Kimberly enlisted the help of her sister. She had so many misgivings about picking out the last outfit she would ever buy her daughter. The many times she and Liz had gone shopping they had

♥ He Blew Her a Kiss

never agreed on anything. How was she going to do this without her there? Her sister drove her to the mall and they immediately headed for a shop that her daughter had once worked at. She knew Liz had always liked the clothes there. Kimberly hesitated a moment at the door and whispered, "Liz, you have got to help me here! I have absolutely no idea what to pick." She slowly walked around and began to peruse the racks. Surprisingly fast, she found a pair of khaki pants and a light blue sweater. She showed it to her sister and said, "I don't know if this is what Liz would want but even if I don't get this right, does it really matter?" Still somewhat unsure, she decided to go with what she picked and proceeded to pay for it. Relieved to have accomplished what she had set out to do, they left.

 The funeral served as a grim reminder of how quickly our loved ones can be lost. It was an emotional ordeal for the many friends and family that attended. The outpouring of love was a testament to how much Liz meant to so many. They appreciated all the words of solace and expressions of sympathy but were thankful to put such a painful event behind them. The following day, Kimberly's sister-in-law, Karen, stopped in to check on her. As they sat in the kitchen drinking coffee and talking, Karen told her, "I was going through some pictures last night and I found one of Liz taken last Christmas. I thought you

The Right Choice ♥

might want to see it." She reached into her purse, pulled the picture out, and laid it on the table. Kimberly lovingly picked it up, smiling as she saw Elizabeth sitting happily with her cousins. Suddenly her breath caught in her throat and she couldn't speak. She looked at Karen, who smiled back at her. Liz was wearing a pair of khaki pants and a light blue sweater! Knowing how she and her daughter had never seen eye-to-eye regarding clothes, she felt in her heart that Liz had been with her at the mall and had guided her to the perfect outfit. Kimberly felt the love and warmth radiating from her heart as she pictured Liz in her new outfit looking down with a beautiful smile, confirming her mother had made the right choice.

~ Submitted by Kimberly Wencl

The Letter

Kimberly stopped by the store on her way to work to pick up several copies of *USA TODAY*. She had been looking forward to this day for the past three weeks. She couldn't wait to get settled in at her desk and read the article. Emails had been sent to notify all her friends and family, so she knew they would be reading it as well. All the excitement and buildup began when she received a phone call three weeks prior.

USA TODAY had decided to run an article on off-campus fires involving students. During their extensive research, they had acquired Kimberly's name. It had been almost three years since her daughter Elizabeth had died in a tragic fire. Liz was a student at a nearby college who lived in an apartment with several other roommates.

♥ He Blew Her a Kiss

The paper staff wanted very much to interview Kimberly for the article. After so much despair and grief, she was relieved that something good might possibly come from her loss. She believed if she could help even one student avoid the mistakes made by her daughter, and 61 other college kids who had lost their lives that year in the same manner, then their deaths would not be in vain. It wouldn't bring Liz back, but in Kimberly's eyes it was a chance to honor her daughter's memory.

Flipping the pages, she found the article and began reading. It only took a few moments for an overwhelming sense of sadness to fill her heart. She had mistakenly thought she could handle reading about her daughter's death again. Even after three years it still seemed so senseless. The enthusiasm Kimberly had felt initially faded quickly. She began having a difficult time dealing with all of the raw, painful emotions that once again bubbled up and grabbed her. The prevailing thought in her mind when first approached was that prevention was the key. Above all, she wanted to keep other families from experiencing the loss of another vibrant young adult. But now in retrospect she argued with herself. How could she possibly think that an article recounting her daughter's death could actually make her happy?

Frustrated and mad at herself, Kimberly angrily tossed the papers on the back credenza of her office and tried to put it out of her mind. No matter how hard she tried to forget about it, she was constantly reminded. All day long a steady stream of coworkers kept stopping by requesting to see the paper. They meant well but it was all she could do to maintain her composure. Kimberly fervently wished she had never mentioned the article to anyone. Obviously this was turning out to be one of "those" days. It had been a while since she had experienced one so she assumed she was due, and simply reminded herself that this too shall pass. One lesson she had learned since Liz's death was that you had to feel the pain before it would leave. It had always worked for her in the past and it would work again.

As the day progressed Kimberly focused on her job. She had taken this position just three weeks after Liz's death. God in his infinite goodness had provided the perfect job at the perfect time. The stress level was low and, because she worked with international customers, the time difference dictated communication via email rather than phone calls. She could come to work, answer all her emails, and then go home. It all worked out perfectly. As Kimberly worked her way through the sea of emails that day, a familiar address caught her attention. It was her daughter's high school French teacher. Jan had been Liz's favorite teacher and kept in touch with Kimberly after the tragic loss.

♥ He Blew Her a Kiss

Assuming Jan was responding to the article Kimberly had notified her about, she hesitated to open it. Reluctantly she proceeded. And much to her relief, there was no mention of USA TODAY or the article. The message she read was, "Kim, you will just treasure this. I was in my classroom yesterday clearing out my files and getting ready for a new school year when a lone file folder fell on the floor. I reached down and picked it up and on the outside it said, *Liz Wencl Essay*. I opened it up and discovered an assignment I had given out more than four years ago. The assignment was to write a letter to one of your parents in French, telling them what they represent in your life. Kim, this is a letter Liz wrote to you!"

Dear Mom,

I know that you love me. You show me each day that it is true. Don't think you are a bad mother. It isn't true! When I look at you I realize how much I am loved.

When you are feeling bad, don't forget – I truly love you. I would like to be a better daughter. We argue sometimes and that makes me sad. I feel bad and unhappy if you cry.

I remember when I was little and you would hug me and say, "I love you so much, Lizzie, sit here with

The Letter ♥

me for just a little while." Those times were so special for me and you made me so happy. I felt like nothing could ever hurt me. I used to wish those moments would never end. To be cuddled up next to you like that today would be like a dream come true.

Mom, I feel sad when you feel sad. And, when you are happy, I am happy! You are my mother and I would never choose anyone else. Without you, I would never be who I am.

I love you with all my heart.

Kisses,
Liz

That letter was a parent's dream. After reading those precious words, Kimberly's difficult day melted away and became a completely amazing day. Once again she was sending an email to friends and family, this time to share the wonderful letter that she had been so blessed to receive. Now Kimberly couldn't wait to get home and share this with her husband. She knew he would appreciate it as well. Finishing her work, she quickly headed home, her heart once again filled with love and joy.

That evening the doorbell rang and she welcomed Liz's teacher into her home. Jan had been thoughtful enough to bring Kimberly the actual letter. As Jan placed

♥ He Blew Her a Kiss

it in Kimberly's hand, she exclaimed, "You have got to know this was no accident." Kimberly quickly replied, "Oh Jan, believe me I do know that!" Jan then proceeded to share how she remembered telling Liz what a beautiful letter it was, and how she had encouraged her to share it with her mother. Liz's profound response was, "I will when the time is right."

Kimberly knew it was no coincidence that Jan had found the letter when she did. She believed with all her heart that Liz was still with her and knew the type of day her mother was going through. Liz had reached out to her in a way that spoke volumes about just how much she loved her mother and missed her. That letter meant the world to Kimberly. It became a physical and tangible symbol of the loving bond she felt with her daughter.

With great pride, Kimberly framed her daughter's words. She had the original letter in French, the translated version in English, and in between was a picture of Liz.

Prominently displayed in their living room, it is a constant reminder of the power of their love. It serves as visual proof for her that Liz reached out and touched her on a day she needed her most. Now, Kimberly accepts that there will be more sad days in the years to come. This time when the sadness threatens to overshadow her, all she will have to do is read her letter and once again feel the strong bond of love they will always share. Kimberly

The Letter ♥

has faith that Liz will always be there for her. In her heart and mind she will always cherish their bond of love that can never be broken, not even by death. As Kimberly so eloquently puts it, "Just as God's love for his children never changes, the love that my daughter and I share never changes. It will live for all eternity."

~ Submitted by Kimberly Wencl

A Gift for Grandpa

Sunday morning had finally arrived! Excitement compelled Kim to rise from the comforting confines of her bed. Today her enthusiasm could not be curbed as her well-planned preparations came to fruition. The family would be celebrating their patriarch's 80th birthday in a relatively short while. Tom Baldwin, normally one to shy away from ostentatious attention, had agreed in good nature to go along with their plans.

Kim made every effort to celebrate her father's life in grand fashion. She had been successful in persuading the local news station to recognize him on their 10 pm broadcast. Likewise, the newspaper ran the announcement of his birthday complete with a photo. Their church, in turn, honored Tom by dedicating the flowers at the altar to this

♥ He Blew Her a Kiss

milestone event. The day was setting up to be quite a memorable one, just as Kim had intended.

Later, the family gathered at the restaurant to celebrate. Earlier that week, Kim had attempted to reserve a private room but to no avail. Slightly disappointed, she vowed not to let that dampen the party. Much to her surprise they were led into a private room after all. Elated that their celebration wouldn't be disturbing others, they were free to laugh and carry on. Two of Kim's favorite cousins, Dawn and Beth, were also in attendance because of close ties to her dad. Beth spent the evening preserving special moments on camera, which seemed only fitting since she worked for a photographer.

The meal was topped off with an extravagant chocolate dessert. Then the assembled family, as if on cue, raised their glasses to toast the man of the day. Tom couldn't contain his happiness as his ear-to-ear grin betrayed him. Struggling valiantly to stem off any tears, he was able to express the deep love and pride he felt for his family. The evening came to a close with hugs for everyone. Beth, anxious to capture her last photo, gathered everyone together. Tom stood proudly surrounded by those that loved him. Each face grinned happily as the camera clicked on the count of three.

All Kim had hoped for fell into place. But despite the happiness of the day, she couldn't help feel a stabbing

A Gift for Grandpa ♥

tinge of sadness. The only thing that kept it from being a perfect day was the absence of her daughter Elizabeth. The 20-year-old college student had died in a tragic fire the fall of 2003. Even though almost nine years had passed, the empty chair at family functions served as a despondent reminder of their heartfelt loss.

The next day Beth sent her cousin Kim an email thanking her for the invitation. She included some of the photos taken the prior evening. Beth also mentioned her initial concern regarding the photographs. The first one she downloaded had a very distinct spot just above Kim's head and positioned on her husband's arm. Beth was afraid the spot would ruin every photo. To her relief, it had only appeared on the one group picture. The longer she examined it, the clearer her deduction became. The spot was positioned in the exact place Elizabeth would have been standing had she been there. Could it possibly be? Knowing Kim had experienced some incredible occurrences after her daughter's death, Beth could not rule out her conclusion.

When Kim finished the email, there was no doubt in her mind. What a wonderful gift to know that Elizabeth had been present for her grandfather's birthday after all. Thrilled with this knowledge, she immediately phoned her father and asked him to stop by. She told him she had one last gift for him.

♥ He Blew Her a Kiss

Upon arriving, Tom entered the kitchen gently scolding his daughter. "Kimmie, I don't need any more birthday presents! Everything you gave me yesterday was wonderful." Kim, smiling like a Cheshire cat, replied, "Oh, I think you'll want this one, Dad, but you'd better sit down first."

Her father complied, sitting at the kitchen table with a puzzled look on his face. Kim placed Beth's email in front of him. As he slowly read the message, the emotion began to show on his face. He set the paper down as Kim silently placed the photo before him. Her father stared for a few minutes and then was overcome by his emotions as he realized the true significance of the spot. Father and daughter shed tears of joy at the thought of Elizabeth being right there with them on such a special day. They hold staunchly to the belief that love never dies, and the bond shared with those we love is never broken…not even by death!

~ Submitted by Kimberly Wencl

A Ride to Remember

Joe stuffed his duffle bag barely thinking about what he was packing. His wife Sue normally shared this task with him, but that would no longer be. Sue had succumbed to her battle with cancer two days earlier and he had to get away. He didn't know where he was going and honestly wasn't very concerned about that. He just needed to get away and take the time to gather himself. Sue had been more than just his wife. They were partners in life. She always had his back and fully supported him in whatever he did. He loved Sue with all his heart and he wasn't sure how he would make it without her. Joe was large in stature. In fact, one of Sue's pet names for him was "Big Guy." And although he might appear rough and tough on the outside, inside he was a very tender-hearted

♥ He Blew Her a Kiss

man. Right now, though, his heart was broken and he felt the need to ride.

Joe cranked his Harley and pulled out of the drive. With no destination in mind, his journey began. As each hour passed, the miles of pavement took him farther and farther from Memphis. Before he knew it, he crossed the state line into Texas. It was then that he stopped. He knew there was something he needed to do. Texas is one state that does not have a helmet law, so, as tribute to Sue he reached into his bag and pulled out her Betty Boop bandana. He tied it on his head and wheeled off again. He knew Sue would approve and he felt even closer to her now. By the time he arrived in San Antonio, he was sweaty and tired. It had been a long ride. He parked his bike, removed the bandana soaked with sweat and hung it on the mirror. It seemed like a cool place to keep it. He checked into a room, cleaned up, and sunk into bed.

The next day Joe inquired if there was a good place around to ride and he was told to head to "Three Sisters," so off he went. For 450 miles, he rode as if on a mission, hard and fast. The wind whipped by him as the music played on the stereo. His bike climbed and descended the overgrown hills that weren't quite mountains but not flat either. Then one of "their" songs came on and he could feel the tears welling up in his eyes. Just as they began to fall, he took a turn just a little too fast. He managed to keep the bike upright but it was enough to slow him down a bit. When he regained his composure, he looked down and Betty Boop was looking right at him. Some sense of familiarity hit him and he just looked up and said, "Thanks for looking after me, honey."

Later that night, as the ride was ending, he exited off the highway and worked his way into town. Traffic began to build, hindering his progress. He rolled up to a stoplight directly behind an SUV. Right in his face at eye level, he read what someone had written on the back window: "Hey Big Guy – Miss You Already." Joe almost died. He was completely taken aback by what he saw. All the way back to the hotel, he kept shaking his head in disbelief. After getting cleaned up, he went back out to get some dinner. Once again he found himself behind another SUV at a stoplight, and this one also had a message drawn on the back window. This one said "Hey Big Sexy!" Okay, he thought, this can't be just coincidence. He realized for whatever reason he had to take this getaway, everything felt okay now. He decided with confidence he could head back home tomorrow, refreshed and composed. It was as if Sue was giving him clues to let him know she was still very much a part of his life.

The next day felt a little brighter as he coasted on to the road home. Riding for hours, he found himself about 50 miles south of Texarkana. Looking ahead, he could

♥ He Blew Her a Kiss

see lightning streaking through the sky. Immediately Sue came to mind. No one loved a storm more than she did. Fascinated with the thunder and lightning, she made it a habit to watch a storm every chance she got, no matter what time of day or night they arrived. He had known her to climb out of bed at three in the morning, excited to see the light show. Suddenly, a loud boom crackled over his head as the lightning seemed to fork on either side of him. Startled, he jumped at the noise. He began to get a little worried but then he just started laughing. He yelled out to the sky, "I know you love storms and you're just playing with me now!" He also told her that if she wanted him, he was ready to come home to her at any time!

The rain began to fall but Joe kept riding. It didn't feel half bad. After all, he was hot and sweaty from the drive so he appreciated what seemed to be a brief cool down from the heat. Then the rain got harder and harder until he realized it wasn't rain anymore, it was hail. The wind kicked up to between 50 to 60 mph. "Okay, Sue, you've got my attention now for sure." His speed had been reduced to 20 mph and he definitely had his flashers on for safety. His eyes strained to spot refuge. After making a mistake in reading his GPS, he missed the only overpass he could have received protection from during the increasing storm. Strangely, after what seemed like only a minute, the sky cleared. It was quite surreal, as if

A Ride to Remember ♥

he had gone through a tunnel with the storm on one end and bright sunny skies on the other. It was then that Joe realized Sue had been with him the entire ride and looking after him.

Joe was glad to make it home and this time it didn't feel quite so lonely. After he had settled in at the house, his phone rang. On the other end was his son Nick. He told his dad he was glad he was home but then he said, "Dad, I know it sounds weird but last night everything was off and the house was quiet when a voice woke me up. I heard 'I love you, Nick.' And Dad, it was Mom's voice. I know it was her." After his own adventure, Joe had no problem believing his son. The trip he had so desperately needed not only served to help him gather his thoughts and regain composure, it also did something he didn't think could be possible. Through those few days he felt closer to Sue than he ever had. It was on an entirely different level, though. He knew life would never be like it used to be when she was physically here with him. However, Sue showed him through little things that she would never be far away. And when you think about it, it's the little things that make a relationship strong. Joe was thankful for her love and grateful to know she still had his back no matter what.

~ Submitted by Joe Moscon

New Beginning

The bond between husband and wife can be one of the strongest connections we experience. This is especially true for couples that have been together for a number of years. Living with someone day in and day out provides the perfect opportunity to discover their true nature. Through all of life's ups and downs it is impossible to hide who you truly are. Many couples become so close they can seemingly read each other's thoughts and can intuitively anticipate the other person's needs. Because of this tie, our spouse so often becomes our best friend. They are one of the few people that know us inside and out. The mere fact they have remained with us over the test of time proves their love is genuine.

♥ He Blew Her a Kiss

Joe and Sue enjoyed just such a relationship. The trust and dependency on one another that had developed through the years was the biggest reason her cancer had been such a devastating blow. Joe wasn't ready to lose his best friend and love of his life. For so long, Sue had been the one to stand by him. She was his moral support, his guiding light, and he lived solely to care for her and keep her happy. In Joe's eyes his wife deserved the best, but this horrible intruder in their lives was something not even he could protect her from.

After learning of her diagnosis, they spent as much time as possible together. Oftentimes, they talked about what was going to happen and Sue tried as best she could to reassure him he would be just fine. She knew what inner strength her husband possessed. She just had to figure out a way for him to find it. During one of their conversations a short time before she passed, Joe was feeling particularly down and began questioning God as to why his wife had to suffer. He felt like it should have been him. Attempting to justify his belief, he quickly explained how she was younger, more beautiful, and still had so much to live for. He also cited many reasons why all of this was wrong and unfair. Sadly, his heart begged for understanding. With a compassionate smile Sue looked into his eyes and said, "There are still things you need to do here. I don't know what, but He will know." Sue's gentle answer

New Beginning ♥

reflected her belief that God had a purpose for everything, including this.

Joe tried to understand his wife's message but, nearly a month after Sue had passed, he still struggled with accepting her loss. Her words echoed repeatedly in his head. With some sense of guilt at not being able to save her, he questioned why he was still here and she was gone. Once before, he had found peace and comfort on a soul-searching trip taken immediately after Sue passed. He thought perhaps a ride would help now as well. Being on his Harley seemed to remove all the pressures and strain from his daily routine. It was an opportunity to find that inner strength he possessed within himself.

So, off Joe cruised with nothing but nature and his thoughts to keep him company. As he pondered what he was going to do with what was left of his life, he was startled by a very clear voice. It was a voice he easily recognized. Sue chastised him in a very loving but firm voice, "Look, I'm dead, you're not! Move on!" Her instructions came with such strength and authority, and Joe knew from past experience that he'd better listen. He tried to join Sue in her belief God still had something planned for him. He was old enough to know he couldn't let grief and pity take control of his life. Once again, he embraced his wife's presence and gained strength and focus from her words.

♥ He Blew Her a Kiss

Four days after Joe's ride, he was walking into their kitchen. Standing against one wall loomed a red hutch with knickknacks decorating its shelves. He immediately chuckled as he recalled how Sue always referred to it as "the red thing." Then something caught his eye. One picture frame in particular was tipped over. He thought that was strange since nothing else seemed to be disturbed. He walked over and set it back upright. Pausing, he began to read the little note inside. It said, "Our God of new beginnings and second chances." Incredibly enough, Joe had walked past this hutch every day, never really noticing the items. Sue knew the message contained there was just what he needed at that time and purposely drew his attention to it.

Joe took a moment to reflect on the message, realizing just how appropriate the words had become at this particular point in his life. Connecting with the sentiments expressed about starting over, he made a resolution right then and there. He was going to embrace this new beginning and see what God and Sue had in store for him. For Joe, the simple note that had escaped his attention for years had turned out to be yet another tool for his wife to use. In his mind, this was a blessing from Sue to put his memories of her and the pain of her loss in their appropriate place and move forward. He understood life must continue and with the comfort and reassurance Sue had so purposefully relayed, he knew he could count on her support. Determined not to let her efforts go in vain, Joe silently vowed to embark on this journey of new beginnings.

~ Submitted by Joe Moscon

A Morning Surprise

It had been almost two months since Joe's wife Sue had passed. Solitude had taken a new identity, one similar to the infamous Dr. Jekyll and Mr. Hyde. Some days it was a warm recollection of all the good times with his wife. But then other days, the solitude weighed so heavy on him that it threatened his very sanity. He knew it would just take time to grow accustomed to being alone after all these years. He was eternally grateful for her love and encouragement, being privileged enough to have received several signs. They were always at difficult times when he really longed for her presence. But try as he might, moving forward with his life was proving to be a daunting task.

One way Joe held on to his sanity was to continue with everyday routines as he had for so many years. Like

♥ He Blew Her a Kiss

slipping on a pair of well-worn shoes, it fit him comfortably. Although sadness lingered around him, especially at home, keeping active helped minimize the pain of her absence. One evening Joe was sitting at home doing nothing specific, his sole companions their three dogs. By ten o'clock, he was tired and ready to go to bed. Climbing to his feet, he proceeded to the door. He always made his rounds inside and outside the house before retiring for the night. The truck was locked up tight but he checked to make sure. Then he did a visual sweep of the carport, including the patio table he and Sue used to sit at every morning. Joe always made sure nothing was left that could blow away during the night. Satisfied all was in order, he went back in the house and locked the door. Last on his list was to check on the dogs, and then he was off to bed.

 Joe and Sue had a specific ritual for greeting each day. Since he was the first to awake around 5:30 am, it was his job to start the coffee. Then he would head outside to the patio table for some alone time. When Sue got up, her coffee was ready and she would join her husband outside with a single cigarette. They would discuss the day ahead, then eventually get moving. So this morning was no different from all the others except that he was alone. He made his coffee and proceeded outside. Walking toward the table he stopped in his tracks. Something didn't feel

A Morning Surprise ♥

right. He couldn't put his finger on it immediately. Could something be in there hiding? He glanced around for a stray raccoon or skunk, but as he surveyed the carport area his eyes fell on the table. There it was. On Sue's side of the table sat a single cigarette.

Now Joe knew it was not there when he'd checked last night. Living somewhat secluded in the country, it was just impossible that someone else had left it there. With disbelief, he approached the table and picked it up. Sue had passed nearly two months ago yet this cigarette was really fresh. Completely filled with amazement, there could be no other explanation for Joe except that Sue had put the cigarette there. Maybe it was just her way of letting him know she was still with him. For sentimental reasons and future inspiration, Joe reverently tucked the cigarette in between pages of her journal for safekeeping.

It wasn't long before their youngest son Luke arrived at the house. Shortly after that, Joe's employees arrived. He sent Luke to retrieve his paperwork out of the shop from the previous day and also gave him the task of washing the truck. Not really expecting answers, Joe began questioning his men about the single cigarette he had found that morning. As he suspected, none of them knew anything about it. So he shared his story to their amazement and, after discussing it a while, sent them off

♥ He Blew Her a Kiss

with a full day of work scheduled. By that time, Luke had finished with the truck and reported back to his dad.

As Joe and his son climbed into the truck, he was surprised to see yet another single cigarette lying on the console. He grabbed it and was just about to throw it out when Luke cried out, "Stop!" Joe asked him why and his son replied, "It's one of Mom's! Can I keep it?" Joe acknowledged it was Sue's but he wanted to know where it had come from. Luke told his father it was the strangest thing. When he went to get the paperwork he had placed on his father's desk the night before, he saw it sitting on top. Joe then asked, "Was it by itself or was there a pack?" Luke responded that it was the only one there. Determined to get to the bottom of these sudden appearances, Joe had the bright idea to replay the footage from his security cameras installed in the shop.

Convinced he would finally get an answer, Joe focused on the video. At the end of the day the paperwork was sitting right where Luke had left it and there was no cigarette. Then the lights went off as the shop was locked up. Fast-forward to the next morning as the lights were turned on, and sure enough, there it was sitting atop the paperwork. No one had entered the shop the entire time. Seeing how much it meant to him, Joe decided to let his son keep the cigarette. Solidly convinced his wife had once again displayed her love and commitment not only

A Morning Surprise ♥

for him but for their son as well, Joe could do nothing but smile to himself. He couldn't explain the strange things that had happened, but he did accept and believe his Sue was behind it all. Her spirit and her love would never be far away, and that was a comforting lift for his saddened heart.

~ Submitted by Joe Moscon

Resources

Support Groups

GriefShare is a grief recovery support group where you can find help and healing for the hurt of losing a loved one. There are thousands of GriefShare support groups meeting weekly throughout the United States and Canada and many groups meeting internationally. GriefShare groups are designed so that you can begin attending on any week. www.griefshare.org

Bereaved Parents of the U.S.A. (BP/USA) is a national nonprofit self-help group that offers support, understanding, compassion, and hope, especially to the newly bereaved, be they bereaved parents, grandparents, or siblings struggling to rebuild their lives after the death of their children, grandchildren, or siblings. www.bereavedparentsusa.org

Compassionate Friends – grief support after the death of a child. Whether your family has had a child die (at any age from any cause) or you are trying to help those who have gone through this life-altering experience, The Compassionate Friends exists to provide friendship, understanding, and hope to those going through the natural grieving process. www.compassionatefriends.org

Resources

Hospice Foundation of America (HFA) – helps people find support groups. www.hospicefoundation.org/supportgroup

National Alliance for Grieving Children (NAGC) – The NAGC promotes awareness of the needs of children and teens grieving a death and provides education and resources for anyone who wants to support them... Because all grieving children deserve a chance to heal. www.childrengrieve.org

Twinless Twins Support Group, International (TTSGI) This group exists to provide a safe and compassionate community for twinless twins to experience healing and understanding. www.twinlesstwins.org

Resources

ADC-Related Websites

www.after-death.com This site is dedicated to After-Death Communication (ADC) experiences and bereavement support for those grieving the death of a loved one.

www.adcrf.org (After-Death Communication Research Foundation) *A website with extensive information and resources regarding after-death communication (ADC), bereavement, grief, and life after death.*

www.oursonbilly.com (Our Son Billy) – Guy and JoAnne Dusseault lost their son Billy in 2003 to a four-wheeler accident. They share their experience along with incredible pictures in which Billy continually communicates with them. Some of the most amazing photos are of heart-shaped moons.

Guy has also launched a Facebook page called "Signs From Our Loved Ones" (www.facebook.com/groups/SignsFromOurLovedOnes), a rapidly growing page where members come together for mutual support and to share signs from their loved ones.

Resources

Books

Hello From Heaven, Bill Guggenheim & Judy Guggenheim. The first book ever written documenting the exciting new field of research on after-death communication.

After-Death Communication, Emma Heathcote-James. Compelling true stories from people who have communicated with their deceased loved one.

Love Lives On: Learning from the Extraordinary Encounters of the Bereaved, Louis E. LaGrand, Ph.D. Dr. LaGrand, a leader in the field of grief counseling, shares insights and true stories from what he calls "Extraordinary Encounters of the bereaved."

Healing Grief, Finding Peace: 101 Ways to Cope with the Death of Your Loved One, Louis E. LaGrand, Ph.D.

Closer Than You Think: The Easy Guide to Connecting with Loved Ones on the Other Side, Deborah Heneghan

But Should the Angels Call for Him: A Mother's Journey through Grief and Discovery, Glenda Pearson, Certified Grief Recovery Specialist

No Reasons for Goodbyes: Messages from Beyond Life, Chassie West

Index

Loss of Child Stories
- A Nugget of Reassurance 9
- In the Line of Duty 23
- A Name Says It All 33
- The Blessing of a Child 45
- Love Shines Bright 55
- Butterfly Kisses 61
- The Journey Begins 93
- Hello, I'm Still Here 101
- The Right Choice 171
- The Letter 177
- A Gift for Grandpa 185

Loss of Grandchild Stories
- A Gift for Grandpa 185

Loss of Grandparent Stories
- Remembering Ma 15
- A Christmas Spirit of Love 65
- A Song of Love 69

211

Loss of Parent Stories

    Morning Glory! Rise and Shine 29
    A Saint's Farewell 39
    The Irises Are Blooming 73
    A Father's Love Is Forever 79
    The Healing House 87
    A Pink Balloon, Please 115
    Love Reflected in a Poem 127
    I Can Always Count on Mom 135
    Wings of Love 143
    Never Far Away 153
    The Beauty of a Butterfly 163

Loss of Sibling Story

    My Hero Forever 119

Loss of Spouse Stories

    He Blew Her a Kiss 1
    A Promise Kept 49
    Fairy-Tale Love 109
    Believe in Yourself 149
    A Ride to Remember 189
    New Beginning 195
    A Morning Surprise 201

About the Authors

Lifelong friends, Angie Pechak Printup and Kelley Stewart Dollar continue their endeavor to help others find comfort while increasing awareness of life after death. Through research and firsthand interviews they have expanded their collection of true accounts regarding after-death communication. Both share the sincere conviction that death is not the end of existence, but merely a transformation. Although skeptics are quick to discredit these experiences as coincidental, Angie and Kelley believe that the proof is undeniable.

CPSIA information can be obtained at www.ICGtesting.com
Printed in the USA
LVOW050739201112

308108LV00001B/7/P

9 781432 791063